M'Liss Rae Hawley's
Round·Robin
Renaissance

 PUBLISHING

Text © 2006 M'Liss Rae Hawley

Artwork © 2006 C&T Publishing, Inc.

Publisher: Amy Marson

Editorial Director: Gailen Runge

Acquisitions Editor: Jan Grigsby

Editor: Darra Williamson

Technical Editors: Teresa Stroin and Nanette Zeller

Copyeditor/Proofreader: Wordfirm, Inc.

Cover Designer: Kristen Yenche

Design Director/Book Designer: Kristen Yenche

Illustrator: Kirstie Pettersen

Production Assistant: Tim Manibusan

Photography: Luke Mulks, Diane Pedersen, and Sharon Risedorph. Author and group photos by Michael Stadler.

Published by C&T Publishing, Inc., P.O. Box 1456, Lafayette, CA 94549

Front cover: *Inside My Garden Gate* (detail) by M'Liss Rae Hawley

Back cover: Border and assorted blocks by the author

Library of Congress Cataloging-in-Publication Data

Hawley, M'Liss Rae

  M'liss Rae Hawley's round robin renaissance / M'Liss Rae Hawley.

    p. cm.

  ISBN-13: 978-1-57120-328-1

  ISBN-10: 1-57120-328-1 (alk. paper)

  1. Patchwork--Patterns. 2. Quilting--Patterns. 3. Friendship quilts. I. Title.

TT835.H34713 2006

  746.46--dc22

2005029446

Printed in China

10 9 8 7 6 5 4 3 2 1

Contents

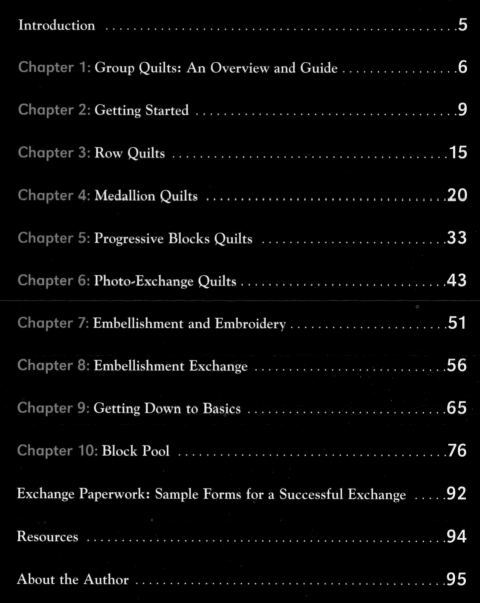

DEDICATION

I lovingly dedicate this book to my best friend, travel companion, and color consultant, but most importantly, my daughter—Adrienne Blythe Hawley.

ACKNOWLEDGMENTS

I would like to thank—both personally and professionally—the following people and companies who share my vision, enthusiasm, and love of quilting, and to express my gratitude for their contributions to the industry.

C&T Publishing: Amy Marson, Jan Grigsby, Darra Williamson, Kristen Yenche, Tim Manibusan, Teresa Stroin, and Kirstie Pettersen.

Hewlett-Packard: Joe Hesch

Husqvarna Viking: Stan Ingraham, Sue Hausmann, Tony Kowal, Nancy Jewell, and Theresa Robinson

In The Beginning Fabrics: Sharon Evans Yenter and Jason Yenter

Hoffman Fabrics: Sandy Muckenthaler

Primedia: Tina Battock and Beth Hayes

Quilters Dream Batting: Kathy Thompson

Robison-Anton Textiles: Bruce Anton and Andreea M. Sparhawk

The Electric Quilt Company: Penny McMorris

I'd also like to express my appreciation to several others without whom this book would not have been possible.

Thanks to Peggy Johnson (the Keeper of the Blocks), who, with software from the Electric Quilt Company, drafted and redrafted the blocks for the book.

And thank you to friends Vicki, Peggy, Susie, and my sister, Erin, for the last-minute help with my bindings.

And finally, a special thank-you to the group of dedicated quilters who agreed to take on yet another project! They inspire me to be a better quilter and writer. We met at Useless Bay Golf and County Club—a beautiful setting with great food. We ate, laughed, argued, and created beautiful quilts.

INTRODUCTION

Inherent in the success (or failure) of traditional round robin quilts is the difference in skill levels of the members. Color preference and selection, accuracy of piecing, and overall workmanship vary, making final assembly a challenge. *Round Robin Renaissance* offers many tips, techniques, and tools for overcoming these challenges and making the group experience a *fun* experience!

The excitement of group quilts lies in the creativity of the shared experience, and *Round Robin Renaissance* presents a fresh, new approach. There is a Block Pool of 30 blocks in various sizes to choose from and five types of quilts to select, some including embroidery and embellishment. For example, each member participating in the Progressive Blocks Quilt constructs the equivalent of two 12″ square (finished) blocks. The quilter may interpret this in a variety of ways by making 2 true 12″ blocks; 8 blocks, each 6″; 18 blocks, each 4″; 32 blocks, each 3″; or a combination of the above. When the blocks are completed by the group, the quilter can assemble them in a traditional method or in a new and innovative way.

In addition to the Progressive Blocks Quilt, you'll find the Photo-Exchange Quilt, which truly reflects the high-tech world in which we live. Cherished images are transferred onto fabric and sent off to the group members to add creative borders. The adventure continues when the bordered blocks are returned to the quilter for assembly.

The Medallion Quilt features a large center block or image surrounded by a series of borders or frames. The instructions for this quilt offer two styles, a straight set and an on-point version. Although this quilt requires a little more planning, it is well worth the effort.

Row Quilts are fast, fun, and easy! The group just exchanges rows of six 6″ blocks. The pieced rows are separated by the background or sashing fabric. This is a great project to work around a theme fabric.

Last but not least—my favorite—a group project that focuses on embellishment! A small wallhanging or pillow is a great way to experiment with new types of surface decoration. The group exchanges strips of fabric, and the members decorate them with a variety of techniques that might include couching, decorative machine stitching, embroidery, raw-edge appliqué, and collage.

Round Robin Renaissance is a guide that offers a new style of round robin quilt. The galleries throughout will inspire and motivate not only groups, but also the individual quilter to make quilts with attitude!

Group Quilts: An Overview and Guide

The concept of quilters working in a group is not new. Quilting bees were formed in the early days of our country's history. Women from all walks of life made quilts together for utility, to commemorate special occasions, or for the sheer beauty of the medium.

Yes, *Round Robin Renaissance* is a book about working with a group—in this case, trading blocks and/or passing a "quilt-in-progress" from hand to hand—and the selection of patterns will get you started. It is also a handbook to inspire and guide you to a successful group experience and to the outstanding quilts that can result from inspired teamwork. But as much as this book is about working within a group, it is also very much about developing your personal artistry. If you are the group leader, once the blocks come back to you, it is up to *you* to design the perfect setting for them. Working with a group is a challenge, but it is also an opportunity! It is a great way to hone your skills in precision cutting and piecing, and perhaps to work with a design or color scheme you might not ordinarily choose on your own. It's a great lesson in creativity and design.

That said, the main advantage of working with a group is the creative exchange between friends. Working together is *fun*! It's a time to relax, quilt, eat, and savor what I call the "reveal"—the moment the finished quilts are shown and shared for the first time.

But I'm getting ahead of myself here. Let's start from the beginning…

> ### Attention, newbies!
> Exchange groups are great for beginners. You'll build confidence in your knowledge of color and design, and build your piecing, quilting, and finishing skills.

THE PERSONALITIES

The first step in your journey into the world of group quilts is to determine who the participants will be. Do you already meet regularly with a small satellite group from your larger quilt guild? Are there quilters in your neighborhood, office, or church community who would enjoy getting together? Is there a quilt shop nearby that might have customers interested in forming a group? Do you have long-distance quilting friends who look forward to meeting at quilt shows or conferences? Perhaps you are a member of an online quilt group. Any of these could form the nucleus of a successful group exchange.

> ### Make new friends!
> Create a group with new members of your quilt guild—it's a wonderful way to help new members feel welcome and get them involved, and for *all* to make new friends.

Next you'll need to decide how many quilters will participate in the exchange. As a general rule of thumb, you'll probably find your group most successful if you keep it somewhere between four and ten members. You don't want the group so small that there are not enough participants, and yet you don't want it so large that there is not enough quilting to go around or that it becomes difficult to handle the logistics of communication and exchange. More on this in Chapter 2 (pages 9–14).

The number of participants in your group may help determine which form of exchange you select from the options presented in this book. While you can certainly modify any of the exchanges to embrace fewer or more members (e.g., the Row Quilt can be adapted to four rows or be increased to include six or seven rows), you will find that certain quilts lend themselves more naturally to larger or smaller groups. The Embellishment Exchange (page 56), for example, is perfect for a small group, while the Progressive Blocks Quilt (page 33) is a good choice for a larger group.

> ### Double the fun!
> If you find yourself with more than ten enthusiastic quilters, consider splitting up into two smaller groups. The groups can work on a parallel schedule, on the same or a different exchange. As an added bonus, you'll have twice the surprise when the quilts are revealed.

Keep in mind that each group is as unique as its members. If you are working with your best friends, you'll want those friendships to be intact at the end of the project. A sense of humor is a prerequisite! Even with all the preplanning in the world, *stuff* is going to happen. Leave your sensitivity at the door.

> ### Stitched with love
> Depending on your style, group quilts may be a challenge for you. Stay focused, do not let blocks and rows, or people and personalities, distract and fragment you. If things get tricky, remember: this is specially chosen fabric stitched with thread by hands that love you!

While you are considering personalities, think about *your* personality as well. How much control do you want over your quilt? Do you want to assign blocks or leave the choices up to the maker? Do you want the other participants to add fabric to yours? Do you want control, or can you let it go? These are decisions you need to make. Find your comfort zone and then make sure it is clear to the others in the group.

Once you have answered these questions, follow through with the best possible guidance for your team. Make sure that you communicate your ideas and wishes clearly. For example, if you want the same background fabric used in every block and have included this fabric in your container (page 10), be sure to label the fabric so there can be no mistake. Each participating quilter should respect the wishes of the originating quilter, but he or she can only do so if the plan is clear.

THE LOGISTICS

Communication is paramount for a successful quilt and a rewarding group experience. If all the participants live near each other, the notes you include with the circulating quilt will be important, but you will also be able to meet and talk to brainstorm ideas and discuss any issues that arise. If your group is a long-distance one, communication will be entirely by phone or in written form (e.g., notes, emails, etc.).

Once the group is formed, consider where, when, and how often you will meet. The first meeting—whether face-to-face or otherwise—is a good time to set guidelines, to determine the format for the exchange (i.e., which project to try), to establish the order of the exchange, and to fill out the forms that will accompany the traveling quilts. Take advantage of this time to share your thoughts, ideas, and *expectations*.

Key in this preliminary discussion is deciding how much time each participant will have to work on the quilt. Be realistic here! Ideally, you'll want to allow each participant a reasonable amount of time to plan and to execute the requirements of the exchange. Aim for deadlines that are neither too short, which place unnecessary pressure on the participants, or too long, which can result in the project losing its "steam." Depending upon the complexity of the exchange project and the other commitments of the group, somewhere between two and four weeks will probably seem appropriate.

If your group is a long-distance one, you must make the same decisions, but with a few additional factors in mind. You'll need to consider how to communicate (phone, email, snail mail), how to move the project from quilter to quilter (postal or other courier service), and how to handle insurance while the project is in transit (to insure or not, and if so, for how much?). You'll also need a schedule that makes accommodation for transit time.

So, this is your challenge. Are you willing to accept it?

Chapter 2

Getting Started

R ound Robin Renaissance offers you an opportunity to grow creatively within the boundaries of another person's quilt. The quilt you are asked to work on may be in a color story or style you are not comfortable with. It may require you to try a block you've never pieced before. Look at this as a time to grow—to experience colors, scale, textures of fabric, and techniques that are new to you.

Once your group is formed, it is time to select the format for your exchange. Will you make Row Quilts or Medallion Quilts? Next, you'll need to determine the location and order of the exchange. Once you've answered these questions, it is up to each quilter to decide on the theme of his or her project, select fabrics, and fill out the Quilters' Guidelines Form (page 92) to inform the others of his or her intentions for the quilt as it passes among the various members.

PREPARING FOR YOUR EXCHANGE QUILT

The Container and Its Contents

Since the blocks and/or quilts-in-progress will be passed from hand to hand, they will need a vehicle in which to make a smooth journey. A roomy clear plastic container makes an excellent choice (see Tip, at right). The chapters describing the five exchanges give specifics as to what the container should include, but in general you'll want to include the following:

- Any existing blocks (e.g., the center block for a Medallion Quilt, embroideries, etc.) or rows to initiate the exchange.

- Any particular fabrics or embellishments you want included in the subsequent blocks or rows. If you want these fabrics used in a particular way (e.g., background, star points, etc.), make sure the appropriate fabrics are clearly identified.

- Diagrams (schematics) of any particular blocks you'd like included in your quilt. You can use the drawings in the Block Pool (pages 76–91) to prepare these diagrams. Simply photocopy them in white, gray, and black if you wish your fellow quilters to follow a certain formula for lights, mediums, and darks. If you have specific preferences as to placement of certain fabrics or colors, trace the block diagram and color as desired. If you have no preference for placement of value, fabric, or color, simply trace the desired blocks and provide uncolored line drawings.

- A completed Quilters' Guidelines Form with contact information, any specific requests or directives for your quilt, the exchange timeline, and so on (see The Paperwork at right for additional information about this form). You'll find a sample form on page 92.

Important!
A plastic container with a lid that seals keeps your paperwork and fabric organized and clean.

The Paperwork

The **Quilters' Guidelines Form** (page 92) is very important. It tells the group about your vision, thoughts, and expectations for your quilt. Take the time to fill it out with care.

The Quilters' Guidelines Form also informs your fellow quilters about how much control you want over the quilt and/or how much freedom they have in making creative choices such as the selection of blocks, fabrics, and so on. Now is the time to consider the following issues:

- How specific do you want to be in terms of the blocks or embellishment techniques used in your quilt? Do you prefer to control all these choices, or are you comfortable leaving these decisions to the participants with just a bit of guidance in terms of your theme, favorite colors, and favorite blocks?

- What fabrics and/or embellishment do you want to include in your container? Do you want to provide all the fabric and trims for your quilt? Will you include only a background and theme fabric? Do you want participants to add fabric and/or embellishments? Do you want the participants to make all the choices?

  These decisions are yours to make and to document on the Quilters' Guidelines Form.

The **Block Log** is extremely helpful for tracking which blocks, in which sizes, are made by each successive quilter. It enables each quilter to easily identify the current state of the quilt and to eliminate duplication of blocks for a more varied result. You'll definitely want to include this form if you have chosen the Progressive Blocks Quilt for your exchange. See page 93 for a sample of the Block Log form.

Technicalities

There are a number of technical issues you will want to resolve before launching the exchange. For example, you will want to be sure that everyone in the group

- uses the same brand of ruler (rulers made by different manufacturers are subject to subtle differences and can vary in their degree of accuracy) and

- agrees to a consistent seam allowance (e.g., $\frac{1}{4}$"-wide rather than a scant $\frac{1}{4}$") and uses the same foot attachment to achieve it.

You will probably think of other technicalities as you meet with your group for the first time to establish the guidelines for your exchange. Make sure that everyone is clear on these decisions. You might even include them in your container as a reminder.

Planning Your Exchange Quilt

As you set the guidelines for your own exchange quilt, begin by "reducing your variables." For example, start with a fabric collection. I used my *Kimono Art Embroidery* collection and coordinating fabric line in my Medallion Quilt (page 20). Barbara Dau began her Progressive Blocks Quilt (page 41) with a collection of hand-dyed fabrics and one background fabric. We both included all the necessary fabric in the container that we passed to each participating quilter.

These fabrics, embroidery designs, and threads provided the inspiration for my quilt *Kimono Art* (page 20).

Another option is to explore a theme. Consider a theme based on your garden, a pet, or the decorative style of a particular room. A patriotic or memorial quilt might commemorate an event or a loved one. Susie Kincy developed her quilt (page 39) around paisleys, both in fabric and embroidery.

Detail of Susie Kincy's quilt A Passion for Paisley (page 39)

HELP YOUR GROUP!

Use your Quilters' Guidelines Form to give the group members as many insights into your intentions for your quilt as possible. You might include key words, such as *traditional, whimsical, sophisticated, bright, country,* or *exotic.* Are you following a color story or using a fabric line and embroidery collection? Have you adopted an ethnic, patriotic, or holiday theme? Are you telling a story with photographs? The more guidance you provide, the better for the participants.

Samples of fabrics used by John James and Susie Kincy to convey the themes in their various exchange quilts

A large-scale book print made the perfect choice as a theme fabric for *No Such Thing* as *Too Many Books* by John James (page 28).

Susie Kincy used an exotic, large-scale floral print for the border of her Hawaiian-themed quilt *Hawaiian Dreams,* and then added fabrics with supporting colors and motifs to enhance her theme (page 24).

Here travel lover Susie Kincy combined a suitcase-bedecked print, a collection of travel photos, and machine embroidery to chronicle her many journeys in her travelogue quilt *Pack Your Bags* (page 49).

When the Exchange Comes to You

Now, the exchange begins!

Whether you are the first or last person in the exchange, your role is equally important.

The first person receives the fabric and notes—and, for example, if the project is the Medallion Quilt, the center block. His or her task is to interpret the information in such a way as to make the best possible choices of blocks and fabric.

The following members of the exchange have a similar task, though they will have blocks, rows, photographs, or sections of a medallion quilt already in progress. The *creation of art* is a process that takes time. Observation and consideration of the details are the keys to success.

Pay attention! When it is your turn, take everything out of the container. Look at the blocks or rows already included, the fabrics (including color, value, and scale of print), any embellishments or photographs, and the notes. Check out what—if anything—has been done before the container has reached you. Let this information guide you. Certain blocks make better choices for particular fabrics and/or themes. Some blocks convey an image through the names they have been given—for example, Birds in the Air or Sister's Choice. Some blocks have a definite diagonal pattern that conveys energy or motion, while other blocks are more "sedate." The choice and size of various filler blocks are considerations too. The goal is to select the blocks and fabrics that best interpret the quilter's story. A thoughtful plan followed by careful attention to the execution of the blocks marks the path to an inspired quilt.

Theme	Diagonal	Filler
Sawtooth Star	Single Irish Chain	Ohio Star
Broken Dishes	Whirlgig	Prairie Queen

BE A PERFECT TEAM MEMBER

Refer to Chapter 9, Getting Down to Basics (pages 65–75), for useful information on constructing blocks and assembling, quilting, and finishing your quilt. Then read through the following tips to ensure that the exchange process moves smoothly.

- Treat any fabric that comes to you as if it were your own. Be conservative (i.e., not wasteful) and respectful in how you use it.

- If the owner of the project does not want you to add fabric, **do not**. If you are welcome to add fabric, prewash it before you incorporate it into the blocks.

- Use 100% cotton thread in colors that blend with the fabrics in the blocks.

- Press your seams as you go. Be consistent! Square up each subunit of the block before proceeding to piece and add additional units.

- Be sure your blocks are the correct size. For example, if a block is to finish 6″ in the quilt, it should measure 6½″ unfinished—that is, when you place it in the container.

- Clean up and carefully square up the blocks as you finish them, making sure to leave a ¼″-wide seam allowance. Clip stray threads on the backs of your blocks.

- Do not sign your blocks unless you are asked to.

- Fill in the Block Log (if appropriate; it's essential for the Progressive Blocks Quilt), add your finished blocks or rows, and return all original materials to the container before passing it on to the next quilter.

EXERCISE DIPLOMACY!

You can choose your fabric and even your blocks... *and* you can choose how you deal with them when they are returned to you. Perhaps they are not exactly what you envisioned. What to do? Remember: these are your friends. Is honesty the best policy? Not if you hurt someone's feelings! Here are some suggestions for gentle feedback when a work in progress is shared with the group and the results are less than expected:

- "You may want to try placing your blocks in this arrangement."

- "I would like to see you try this fabric for your accent border."

- "Your quilt has changed so much since you selected your border fabric. You may want to audition another fabric."

IT'S A WRAP

So you have your blocks, rows, bordered photographs, and/or embellished strips. What to do next? This is where your creativity comes into play! Experiment on graph paper or place the blocks, rows, and units on a design wall to create a set that works for you. Refer to the chapter that describes your exchange (and the beautiful gallery quilts that accompany each one) for possible settings, including suggested yardages for sashing, borders, and so on.

Just remember: the exchange is not finished until the quilts are finished! Plan a reunion. You may find that it begins another exchange. Have fun!

Blocks not all the same size?

There are many creative solutions for solving this dilemma. For example, insert pieced spacer units, such as Checkerboard squares (page 79), Flying Geese units (page 80), Half-Square Triangles (page 81), or Honeycomb units (page 82). Design specially sized embroidered or appliquéd strips to fill the gaps. Sashing and lattice strips present additional creative options. Feel free to adjust the lengths and widths as needed for fit.

Chapter 3

Row Quilts

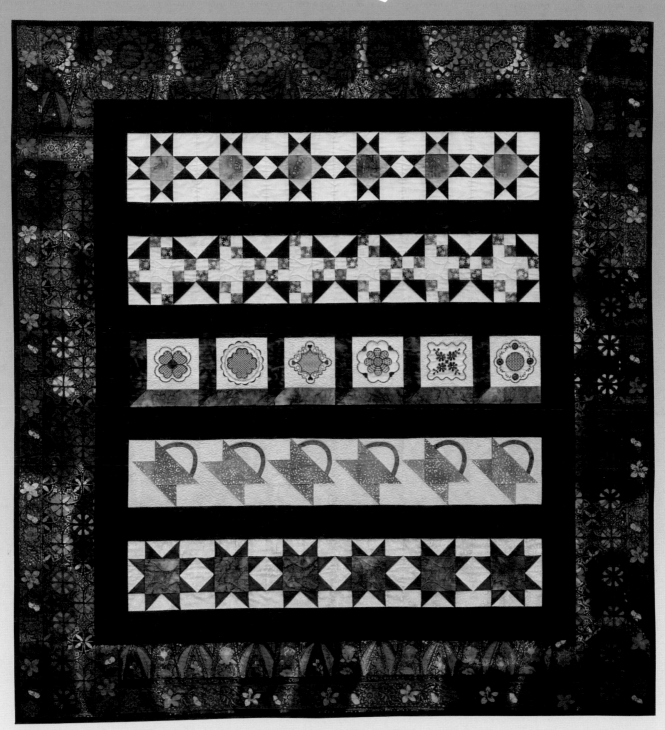

International, 54″ × 60″. Blocks contributed by the group. Designed and assembled by M'Liss Rae Hawley, 2005. Machine quilted by Barbara Dau.

Row quilts—made up of rows of blocks separated by horizontal or vertical sashing—are fast and fun! In fact, they are the easiest form of exchange in this book. Row quilts are so straightforward that they easily adapt to any theme, so a good place to start is by selecting a theme fabric and using it as a guide for the other fabrics in the quilt.

The row quilt format calls for five rows of six blocks each, but you can tailor the number of rows or blocks to suit the needs and wishes of your group. (If you do so, be sure to adjust the yardages and cut sizes of the sashing, borders, batting, backing, and binding.) For *International*, I asked each member of my group to make six of a specific block using the same fabrics in each block. I provided batik fabrics that coordinated colorwise with my border fabric, a handmade batik from Malaysia.

Note: Materials and cutting specifications listed are for sashing, borders, batting, backing, and binding. Materials for individual blocks will depend upon the selection made, and can be found in the Block Pool beginning on page 76. The quilt shown features the 6˝ Ohio Star (page 84), Prairie Queen (page 86), Attic Window (page 77), Party Basket (page 85), and Sawtooth Star (page 87) blocks.

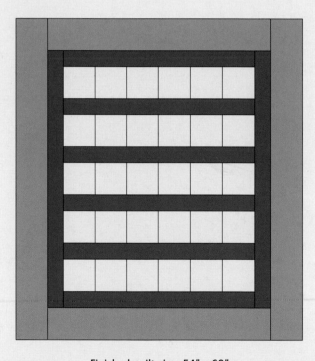

Finished quilt size: 54″ x 60″

MATERIALS

All yardage is based on fabric that is 40˝ wide after laundering.

1 yard for the sashing

1⅓ yards for the border

⅔ yard for the binding

3⅝ yards for the backing

62˝ × 68˝ piece of batting

CUTTING

Cut all strips across the fabric width.

From the sashing fabric:
Cut 9 strips, 3½˝ × 40˝; crosscut 6 strips, 3½˝ × 36½˝.

From the border fabric:
Cut 6 strips, 6½˝ × 40˝.

From the binding fabric:
Cut 7 strips, 3˝ × 40˝.

QUILT ASSEMBLY

Now that you have your rows of blocks, the fun begins!

1. Arrange the rows and the 3½˝ × 36½˝ sashing strips, alternating them as shown in the assembly diagram on page 17. Stitch the rows and sashing together. Press the seams toward the sashing.

2. Piece the remaining sashing strips and stitch to the sides. Press the seams toward the sashing.

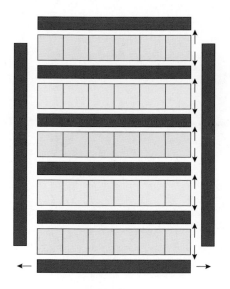

Assembly diagram

3. Refer to Squared Borders (page 68). Measure, trim, and sew a 6½″-wide border strip to the top and bottom of the quilt, piecing as necessary. Press the seams toward the border. Repeat to sew 6½″-wide borders to the sides. Press.

Finishing

Refer to Preparing Your Quilt for Quilting (page 70), Quilting (page 71), and Finishing Your Quilt (page 72).

1. Piece the backing if necessary.

2. Layer the quilt top, batting, and backing; baste.

3. Hand or machine quilt as desired.

4. Use the 3″-wide strips to bind the edges of the quilt.

5. Add a hanging sleeve and label if desired.

 ## Think outside the embroidery box!

I used a candlewicking-based embroidery collection for my row of Attic Window blocks (see Resources, page 94). However, rather than using the traditional white or ecru thread on neutral fabric, I used purple 35-weight rayon thread on a yellow batik.

Detail of *International* (for a full view of this quilt, see page 15)

 ## FAQ (Frequently Asked Questions)

"Must my blocks be 6½″?"

Yes, if that is the decision made by the quilt owner. Each row must finish 36″ (6 blocks × 6″) to fit in the same quilt!

Almost Christmas, 54″ × 60″.
Blocks contributed by the group. Designed and assembled by Peggy Johnson, 2005. Machine quilted by Barbara Dau.

Whidbey in the Fall, 54″ × 60″. Blocks contributed by the group. Designed and assembled by Vicki DeGraaf, 2005. Machine quilted by Barbara Dau.

Rows of Friendship, 54″ × 60″.
Blocks contributed by the group. Designed and assembled by Susie Kincy, 2005. Machine quilted by Barbara Dau.

Christmas Greeting Card, 54″ × 60″.
Blocks contributed by the group. Designed, assembled, beaded, and hand embroidered by Anastasia Riordan, 2005. Machine quilted by Barbara Dau.

Medallion Quilts

Kimono Art, 54″ × 62″. Blocks contributed by the group. Designed and assembled by M'Liss Rae Hawley, 2005. Machine quilted by Barbara Dau.

Medallion quilts are composed of a center block or panel surrounded by a series of borders or frames. The style can be traced back to the late eighteenth century, both in America and in Europe. Although a medallion quilt requires a little more planning, it is well worth the effort. You may select one of two formats: a straight set, which I chose for *Kimono Art*, or an on-point version, which Susie Kincy used for her quilt *Hawaiian Dreams* (page 24).

Begin your Medallion Quilt with a theme or a favorite fabric and create a center block that enhances your choice. Pin your block to the center of a piece of batting, white flannel, muslin, or other design surface large enough to accommodate the quilt top as each successive border is made. Then pack up your center block and portable "design wall," any fabric(s) you'd like to see included, and the necessary paperwork, and pass it all on to the first person in your group.

Each participant in the group constructs a border following any directions and dimensions you've outlined for his or her step in the process. Rather than sewing the finished border to the center block, the quilter pins the border to the design surface in the appropriate position. When the work is returned to the owner—you!—it's your task to put the quilt top together, adding the desired inner and outer borders.

For *Kimono Art* (page 20), I started by making a 12″ center block, which I framed with a 1″ finished border. Subsequent participants contributed a 4″ pieced border, a 6″ pieced border, and a top and bottom border of 4″ pieced blocks. When the quilt was returned to me, I assembled it, adding four additional "unpieced" borders, including the outer border in an Asian-inspired large-scale leaf pattern.

Note: Materials and cutting specifications listed are for borders, batting, backing, and binding. Materials for individual blocks will depend upon the selection made, and can be found in the Block Pool beginning on page 76. The quilt shown features the 2″ × 4″ Honeycomb block (page 82), the 4″ Broken Dishes block (page 79), and the 6″ Attic Window block (page 77). Refer to the assembly diagrams as needed.

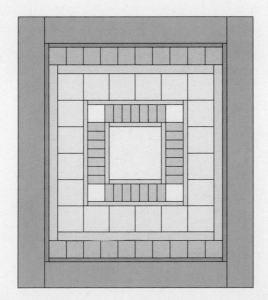

Finished quilt size: 54″ × 62″

MATERIALS

All yardage is based on fabric that is 40″ wide after laundering.

¾ yard for the first (accent), second (accent), and third borders

¼ yard for the fourth (accent) border

1¼ yards for the outer border

¼ yard for the corner stones

¾ yard for the binding

3⅝ yards for the backing

62″ × 70″ piece of batting

CUTTING

Cut all strips across the fabric width.

From the first, second, and third border fabric:

Cut 2 strips, 1½″ × 12½″ (first border).

Cut 2 strips, 1½″ × 14½″ (first border).

Cut 2 strips, 1½″ × 22½″ (second border).

Cut 2 strips, 2½″ × 36½″ (second border).

Cut 3 strips, 2½″ × 40″ (third border).

From the fourth border fabric:
Cut 5 strips, 1½″ × 40″.

From the outer border fabric:
Cut 6 strips, 6½″ × 40″.

From the corner stone fabric:
Cut 4 squares, 4½″ × 4½″.

From the binding fabric:
Cut 7 strips, 3″ × 40″.

Quilt Assembly

1. Sew a $1\frac{1}{2}'' \times 12\frac{1}{2}''$ first border strip to the top and bottom of the $12\frac{1}{2}''$ block. Press. Repeat to sew $1\frac{1}{2}'' \times 14\frac{1}{2}''$ first borders to the sides. Press.

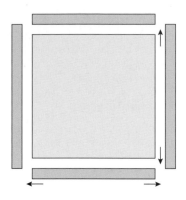

2. Sew seven $2\frac{1}{2}'' \times 4\frac{1}{2}''$ blocks together to make a row. Press. Make 4. Sew a row to the top and bottom of the quilt. Press. Sew a $4\frac{1}{2}''$ corner stone to opposite ends of each remaining row. Press. Sew to the sides. Press.

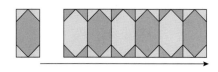

Make 4.

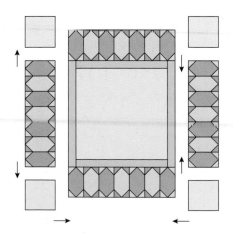

Options, options!

The quilt shown uses $2'' \times 4''$ (finished) Honeycomb blocks for the border between the first two accent borders. If you like, you can substitute $2'' \times 4''$ Flying Geese (page 80), $1''$ Checkerboard squares stacked in sets of 2 (page 79), or $2''$ Half-Square Triangles (page 81).

3. Sew a $1\frac{1}{2}'' \times 22\frac{1}{2}''$ second border strip to the top and bottom of the quilt. Press the seams toward this border. Repeat to sew $1\frac{1}{2}'' \times 24\frac{1}{2}''$ second borders to the sides. Press.

4. Sew four $6\frac{1}{2}''$ blocks together to make a row. Press. Make 2 and sew to the top and bottom of the quilt. Press. Sew six $6\frac{1}{2}''$ blocks together to make a row. Press. Make 2 and sew to the sides. Press.

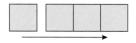

Make 2 of each.

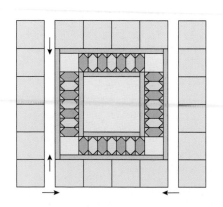

---

5. Sew a $2\frac{1}{2}'' \times 36\frac{1}{2}''$ third border strip to the top and bottom of the quilt. Press the seams toward this border. Repeat to sew $2\frac{1}{2}'' \times 40\frac{1}{2}''$ third borders to the sides, piecing as necessary. Press.

6. Sew ten $4\frac{1}{2}''$ blocks together to make a row. Press. Make 2 and sew to the top and bottom of the quilt. Press.

Make 2.

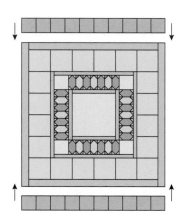

7. Refer to Squared Borders (page 68). Measure, trim, and sew a 1½″-wide fourth border strip to the top and bottom of the quilt, piecing as necessary. Press the seams toward this border. Repeat to sew 1½″-wide fourth borders to the sides. Press.

8. Measure, trim, and sew a 6½″-wide outer border strip to the top and bottom of the quilt, piecing as necessary. Press the seams toward this outer border. Repeat to sew 6½″-wide outer borders to the sides. Press.

FINISHING

Refer to Preparing Your Quilt for Quilting (page 70), Quilting (page 71), and Finishing Your Quilt (page 72).

1. Piece the backing if necessary.

2. Layer the quilt top, batting, and backing; baste.

3. Hand or machine quilt as desired.

4. Use the 3″-wide strips to bind the edges of the quilt.

5. Add a hanging sleeve and label if desired.

Blocks not accurate?

Consider adding sashing, lattice strips, or other spacers to make up the difference.

Dragons on the Wind, 54″ × 62″. Blocks contributed by the group. Designed and assembled by Louise James, 2005. Machine quilted by Barbara Dau.

OPTIONAL ON-POINT MEDALLION SET

Hawaiian Dreams, 54″ × 62″. Blocks contributed by the group. Designed and assembled by Susie Kincy, 2005. Machine quilted by Barbara Dau.

Turning the center block on point gives the Medallion Quilt a different look, as evidenced by Susie Kincy's lovely *Hawaiian Dreams*. With just a few minor modifications in cutting and piecing, the construction is basically the same as the straight-set format I used for *Kimono Art* (page 20). For other on-point medallions, see *Brotherhood of Hope* (page 31), *April Love* (page 28), *Oregon Poinsettias* (page 30), and *Asian Fusion* (page 27).

The schematic below indicates the format Susie followed. She began with the framed 12″ center block. However, instead of adding a border of 4″ blocks, she turned the center block on the diagonal and squared it off with large half-square triangles and a second accent border. The rest of the quilt is constructed following Steps 4–8 on pages 22–23.

Note: Materials and cutting specifications listed are for setting triangles, borders, batting, backing, and binding. Materials for individual blocks will depend upon the selection made, and can be found in the Block Pool beginning on page 76. The quilt shown features the 6″ Kaleidoscope (page 82) and Attic Window (page 77) blocks and 4″ plain and embroidered squares. Refer to the assembly diagrams as needed.

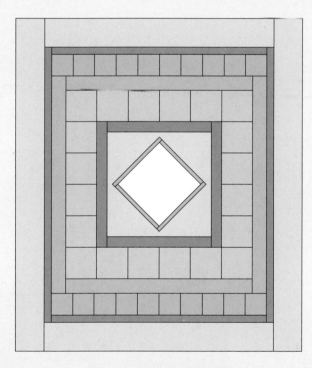

Finished quilt size: 54" x 62"

MATERIALS

All yardage is based on fabric that is 40″ wide after laundering.

¾ yard for the first (accent), second (accent), and third borders

⅜ yard for the corner triangles

¼ yard for the fourth (accent) border

1¼ yards for the outer border

¾ yard for the binding

3⅝ yards for the backing

62″ × 70″ piece of batting

CUTTING

Cut all strips across the fabric width.

From the first, second, and third border fabric:

Cut 2 strips, 1½″ × 12½″ (first border).

Cut 2 strips, 1½″ × 14½″ (first border).

Cut 2 strips, 2″ × 21½″ (second border).

Cut 2 strips, 2″ × 24½″ (second border).

Cut 2 strips, 2½″ × 36½″ (third border).

Cut 3 strips, 2½″ × 40″ (third border).

From the corner triangle fabric:

Cut 2 squares, 11⅜″ × 11⅜″; cut each square once diagonally to yield 2 half-square triangles (4 total).

From the fourth border fabric:

Cut 5 strips, 1½″ × 40″.

From the outer border fabric:

Cut 6 strips, 6½″ × 40″.

From the binding fabric:

Cut 7 strips, 3″ × 40″.

QUILT ASSEMBLY

1. Sew a 1½″ × 12½″ first border strip to the top and bottom of the 12½″ block. Press. Repeat to sew 1½″ × 14½″ first borders to the sides. Press.

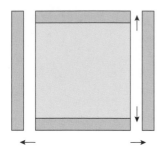

2. Sew a half-square corner triangle to opposite sides of the unit from Step 1. Press. Sew half-square triangles to the remaining sides. Press. Trim the unit to measure 21½″ × 21½″.

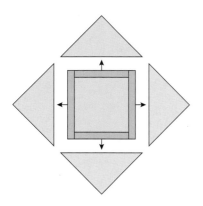

3. Sew a 2″ × 21½″ second border strip to the top and bottom of the quilt. Press the seams toward this border. Repeat to sew 2″ × 24½″ second borders to the sides. Press.

4. Refer to Steps 4–6 page 22 to continue constructing the quilt as shown below and at right.

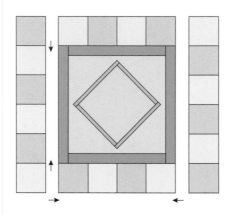

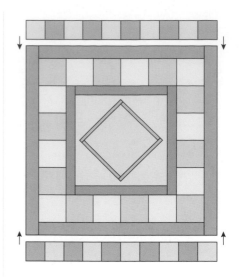

5. Refer to Steps 7 and 8 (page 23) to add the fourth and the outer borders. Follow the Finishing instructions (page 23) to complete the quilt.

Susie opted for a row of 4″ (finished) plain and embroidered blocks for the final pieced border of *Hawaiian Dreams*. For a full view of this quilt, see page 24.

Asian Fusion, 54″ × 62″.
Blocks contributed by the group. Designed, assembled, and machine quilted by Barbara Dau, 2005.

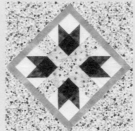

April Love, 56″ × 63″.
Blocks contributed by the group. Designed and assembled by Marie Miller, 2005. Machine quilted by Barbara Dau.

No Such Thing as Too Many Books, 54″ × 62½″.
Blocks contributed by the group. Designed and assembled by John James, 2005. Machine quilted by Barbara Dau.

Gardening Angel, 55″ × 63″.
Blocks contributed by the group. Designed and assembled by Anastasia Riordan, 2005. Machine quilted by Barbara Dau.

Aunt Lucy's Treasure From the Attic, 58″ × 66″.
Blocks contributed by the group. Designed and assembled by Carla Zimmermann, 2005. Machine quilted by Kim McKinnon.

Oregon Poinsettias, 54″ × 62″.
Blocks contributed by the group. Designed and assembled by Annette Barca, 2005.
Machine quilted by Barbara Dau.

Cardinals in the Winter,
54″ × 62″.
Blocks contributed by the group.
Designed and assembled by Stacie
Johnson, 2005. Machine quilted by
Stacie Johnson and Debbie Webster.

Brotherhood of Hope, 54″ × 62″.
Blocks contributed by the group. Designed
and assembled by Leslie Rommann, 2005.
Machine quilted by Barbara Dau.

Evening Star, 54″ × 62″. Blocks contributed by the group. Designed and assembled by Barb Higbee-Price, 2005. Machine quilted by Barbara Dau.

Chapter 5

Progressive Blocks
Quilts

Inside My Garden Gate, 59½″ × 69″. Blocks contributed by the group.
Designed and assembled by M'Liss Rae Hawley, 2005. Machine quilted by Barbara Dau.

his is an exciting exchange, presenting the group members with even greater opportunities to stretch technically and artistically. In this exchange, the participating quilters have considerably more freedom to decide how to interpret the directive, and the originating quilter must work within the parameters of the blocks returned to him or her by the others. With so many choices, quilters of all skill levels can gain from the Progressive Blocks experience.

Here's how the Progressive Blocks Quilt exchange works. The originating quilter establishes a theme and a color story, and perhaps provides some or all of the fabric. Each participating member constructs the equivalent of two 12″ (finished) blocks. This may be interpreted in a variety of ways: by making 2 true 12″ blocks; 8 blocks, each 6″; 18 blocks, each 4″; 32 blocks, each 3″; or a combination of the above. Regardless of their sizes, *don't* sew any of the blocks together.

When all the blocks are returned to the original quilter, the possibilities for creativity are endless. The challenge becomes combining artistry with math. The blocks will be all different sizes, so decisions must be made! Should you combine 3″, 4″, or 6″ blocks to create 12″ blocks? Group 6″ blocks in pairs? Use sashing? Add embroidery? In *Inside My Garden Gate* (page 33), I included embroidery in the Attic Window blocks, in a center square, and in the 3″ × 12″ panels. The vertical orientation enhanced the floral spray and the overall look of the quilt. If you do not have access to an embroidery machine, the space may be filled with four 3″ blocks.

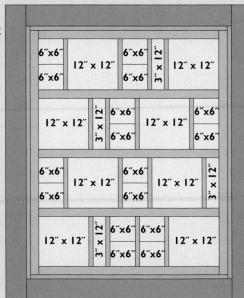

Finished quilt size: 59 1/2″ x 69″

Whatever the answers to these questions, this is a moment to move from the mundane to the inspired. Let creativity be your guide.

 FAQ (Frequently Asked Questions)

"What is the difference between the Progressive Blocks Quilt and the Row Quilt (page 15)?"

Although the two have some similarities, what differentiates the Progressive Blocks Quilt from the Row Quilt is the opportunity to take individual blocks and use them to create new, exciting, and original layouts. Rather than receiving a set of preconstructed *rows*, you receive *blocks* that you can combine into all types of sampler sets—in vertical or horizontal rows, with or without sashing and corner stones, in medallion arrangements, with filler strips and/or blocks.

Take time to study your blocks. Do they meet your expectations? Do they complement the feel of your theme fabric? (Are they better than you could have imagined?)

Note: Materials and cutting specifications listed are for sashing, borders, batting, backing, and binding. Materials for individual blocks will depend upon the selection made, and can be found in the Block Pool beginning on page 76. The quilt shown features the 2″ × 4″ Flying Geese block (page 80); the 6″ Attic Window (page 77), Birds in the Air (page 78), Kaleidoscope (page 82), Prairie Queen (page 86), Sawtooth Star (page 87), and Useless Bay (page 90) blocks; and the 12″ Autumn Leaf (without a stem—page 77), Pink Magnolia (page 85), Sister's Choice (page 88), Tumbling Star (page 89), and Waterwheel (page 90) blocks. Refer to the diagram at left as needed.

And now for something different!

Note that I substituted a 4″ Pink Magnolia embroidered square for a plain square in the center of the Flying Geese–framed block in the lower right corner of *Inside My Garden Gate* (page 33). See Resources on page 94 for this and other embroidery patterns used in this quilt.

For a full view of this quilt, see page 33.

MATERIALS

All yardage is based on fabric that is 40″ wide after laundering.

⅞ yard for the sashing

¼ yard for the accent border

1⅓ yards for the outer border

⅞ yard for the binding

4 yards for the backing

68″ × 77″ piece of batting

 ## Look at the theme fabric!

Let it guide you to appropriate block and fabric choices.

CUTTING

Cut all strips across the fabric width.

From the sashing fabric:
Cut 6 strips, 1½″ × 40″; crosscut 16 strips, 1½″ × 12½″.

Cut 9 strips, 2″ × 40″.

From the accent border fabric:
Cut 6 strips, 1¼″ × 40″.

From the outer border fabric:
Cut 6 strips, 6½″ × 40″.

From the binding fabric:
Cut 8 strips, 3″ × 40″.

QUILT ASSEMBLY

1. Refer to the diagram on page 34 and the assembly diagram at right. Arrange two 6½″ × 12½″ units, two 12½″ × 12½″ blocks or units, a 3½″ × 12½″ unit, and four 1½″ × 12½″ sashing strips in each of the 4 horizontal rows as shown. Sew the units, blocks, and sashing strips together. Press.

2. Sew the 2″-wide sashing strips together end to end. Cut 5 strips, 2″ × 43½″. Arrange the 2″ × 43½″ strips and the rows from Step 1, alternating them as shown in the assembly diagram. Sew the strips and rows together. Press.

3. Cut 2 strips, 2″ × 56″, from the remaining 2″-wide strip. Sew to the sides of the quilt. Press.

4. Refer to Squared Borders (page 68). Measure, trim, and sew a 1¼″-wide accent border strip to the top and bottom of the quilt, piecing as necessary. Press the seams toward the border. Repeat to sew 1¼″-wide accent borders to the sides. Press.

5. Measure, trim, and sew a 6½″-wide outer border strip to the top and bottom of the quilt, piecing as necessary. Press the seams toward the outer border. Repeat to sew 6½″-wide outer borders to the sides. Press.

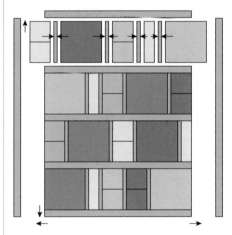

Assembly diagram

FINISHING

Refer to Preparing Your Quilt for Quilting (page 70), Quilting (page 71), and Finishing Your Quilt (page 72).

1. Piece the backing if necessary.

2. Layer the quilt top, batting, and backing; baste.

3. Hand or machine quilt as desired.

4. Use the 3″-wide strips to bind the edges of the quilt.

5. Add a hanging sleeve and label if desired.

Permission!

You have "permission" not to use a block that is made for you if it doesn't work in the quilt top. Instead, you might incorporate the block into the quilt backing or use it to make the quilt label or a pillow. Depending upon your group, you may also ask the maker to piece an alternate block.

Asian Sampler, 61″ × 76″.
Blocks contributed by the group. Designed and assembled by Stacie Johnson, 2005. Machine quilted by Stacie Johnson and Debbie Webster.

Blue and White Medallion, 52″ × 65″.
Blocks contributed by the group. Designed and
assembled by Annette Barca, 2005. Machine
quilted by Barbara Dau.

Coffee Sampler, 53″ × 66″.
Blocks contributed by the group.
Designed and assembled by Louise
James, 2005. Machine quilted
by Barbara Dau.

See What My Friends Did, 30″ × 54″.
Blocks contributed by the group. Designed and
assembled by Leslie Rommann, 2005. Machine
quilted by Arlene Anderson.

Playing With Progressive Blocks,
59″ × 59″.
Blocks contributed by the group. Designed
and assembled by Carla Zimmermann, 2005.
Machine quilted by Patsi Hanseth.

A Passion for Paisley, 68″ × 86″.
Blocks contributed by the group. Designed and assembled by Susie Kincy, 2005.
Machine quilted by Barbara Dau.

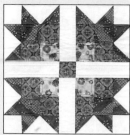

Blue Kabuki, 56″ × 60″. Blocks contributed by the group. Designed and assembled by Anastasia Riordan, 2005. Machine quilted by Barbara Dau.

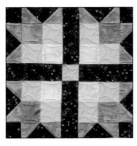

Evening Sparkle, 54″ × 64″.
Blocks contributed by the group.
Designed, assembled, and machine
quilted by Barbara Dau, 2005.

Holiday Elegance, 69″ × 55″.
Blocks contributed by the group.
Designed and assembled by Marie
Miller, 2005. Machine quilted by
Barbara Dau.

Bring in the Clowns, 50″ × 55″.
Blocks contributed by the group. Designed
and assembled by John James, 2005.
Machine quilted by Barbara Dau.

Spring View Fun, 63″ × 92″.
Blocks contributed by the group. Designed
and assembled by Barb Higbee-Price, 2005.
Machine quilted by Barbara Dau.

Photo-Exchange Quilts

Where's George? 35˝ × 41˝. Blocks contributed by the group. Designed and assembled by M'Liss Rae Hawley, 2005. Machine quilted by Barbara Dau. Photos by Michael A. Hawley.

The Photo-Exchange project is a wonderful opportunity to make a quilt with cherished photographs. The potential for subject matter is endless. You might choose to highlight family activities such as sports, vacations, or special events. John James paired prized photographs from his military career in his quilt *Harriers* (page 45), while Annette Barca designed a memory quilt, *Love You, Tyler: 1990–2005* (page 49), with cherished photos of her great nephew, Tyler. Anastasia Riordan created a triptych, *Russian Meditation* (page 50), to showcase images from a trip to Russia.

I selected our garden here on Whidbey Island, Washington, as the subject for my Photo-Exchange Quilt. My husband, Michael, and I are avid gardeners, and he takes many photographs of our flowers and orchards. I used the Attic Window block (page 77) to showcase the photographs and then asked the group to echo the Attic Window image with Log Cabin blocks (page 83). Finally, I used a Japanese fabric with a floral motif for the border.

I incorporated these photos taken by my husband, Michael, into *Where's George?* (page 43) and framed the quilt with a complementary floral print.

Your group can approach this exchange in different ways. Plan a gathering (physical, via snail mail, or in cyberspace) to consider the following possible options:

- Place your photographs in the exchange container along with the fabric and let the group members decide how to proceed—if and how to border the photos and what (if any) pieced blocks to add.

- Hold on to your photographs and suggest blocks for the group to make that will complement your theme. Encourage the participants to be observers of the images, the theme, and fabric and to let these act as guides.

- Compose the center of the quilt yourself, and then have members make border blocks. This is the strategy Louise James used for her quilt *Foraging for Mushrooms* (page 47).

Whatever the subject matter or the approach for your particular exchange, remember that you are all sharing an important part of your lives through the images you select. Be sure to keep the intimacy of the images the focus of the quilt.

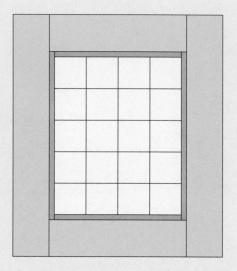

Finished quilt size: 35˝ x 41˝

Note: Materials and cutting specifications listed are for borders, batting, backing, and binding. Materials for individual blocks will depend upon the selection made, and can be found in the Block Pool, beginning on page 76. The quilt shown features the 6˝ Log Cabin (page 83) and Attic Window (page 77) blocks, with a 5˝ × 5˝ photo transfer replacing piece B in each Attic Window block. Refer to the assembly diagram as needed.

MATERIALS

All yardage is based on fabric that is 40˝ wide after laundering.

¼ yard for the inner border

⅞ yard for the outer border

½ yard for the binding

2½ yards for the backing

43˝ × 49˝ piece of batting

CUTTING

Cut all strips across the fabric width.

From the inner border fabric:
Cut 4 strips, 1˝ × 40˝.

From the outer border fabric:
Cut 4 strips, 5½˝ × 40˝.

From the binding fabric:
Cut 5 strips, 3˝ × 40˝.

QUILT ASSEMBLY

1. Refer to the assembly diagram below. Arrange the 6½˝ blocks in 5 horizontal rows of 4 blocks each. Sew the blocks together. Press. Sew the rows together. Press.

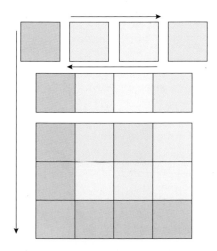

Assembly diagram

2. Refer to Squared Borders (page 68). Measure, trim, and sew a 1˝-wide inner border strip to the top and bottom of the quilt. Press the seams toward the border. Repeat to sew 1˝-wide inner borders to the sides. Press.

3. Measure, trim, and sew a 5½˝-wide outer border strip to the top and bottom of the quilt. Press the seams toward the outer border. Repeat to sew 5½˝-wide outer borders to the sides, piecing as necessary. Press.

FINISHING

Refer to Preparing Your Quilt for Quilting (page 70), Quilting (page 71), and Finishing Your Quilt (page 72).

1. Piece the backing if necessary.

2. Layer the quilt top, batting, and backing; baste.

3. Hand or machine quilt as desired.

4. Use the 3˝-wide strips to bind the edges of the quilt.

5. Add a hanging sleeve and label if desired.

Harriers, 40˝ × 40˝. Pieced blocks contributed by the group. Designed and assembled by John James, 2005. Machine quilted by Barbara Dau.

PHOTO TRANSFER

There are a number of excellent books about transferring photos to fabric. I have included some of my favorites in Resources on page 94. I've also included some suggestions on where to find pretreated fabric sheets. Meanwhile, here are some tips and ideas to get you started.

Samples of products available for transferring photos to fabric

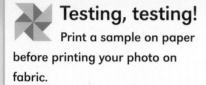

Testing, testing!

Print a sample on paper before printing your photo on fabric.

Printing on Fabric

1. Check your fabric sheet before printing to be sure it is wrinkle free. If you must press, don't use steam. This may cause water spots or cause the fabric to separate from the paper backing.

2. Printers don't print the color white. The white parts of the image will be the same color as your fabric. Also keep in mind that the inks are transparent, so the fabric color may affect the print colors.

3. Check your printer's manual to determine how to feed the fabric sheets (one at a time) into your printer.

4. Make sure the leading edge of the fabric is securely bonded to the backing paper. If the fabric has separated, use masking tape or stitch around the top edge with a short stitch length.

5. Trim—don't pull—loose threads from the fabric sheet before inserting it into the printer.

6. Leave at least a ¼″ allowance on all 4 sides of your image for a seam allowance.

7. Allow the ink to dry completely before removing the paper backing.

8. Follow the manufacturer's recommendations for setting and/or rinsing the fabric sheet before you start your project.

Ready, Set, Print!

Here is how it works on my computer (and many others).

1. Open the file you want to print.

2. Select **Print** from the **File** menu.

3. Choose **Properties**.

4. Under **Print Quality**, choose **Best** or **High**.

5. For **Paper** or **Media Type**, choose **Plain**.

6. Click **OK** to accept the settings.

7. Click **OK** to start printing.

And there you go!

Need Photos?

Here are some ideas for photo sources:

- Scan photos from your photo albums, slides, or negatives.
- Print images from your photo CD or from a copyright-free photo collection.
- Download photos from copyright-free websites.
- Scan three-dimensional objects such as flowers, lace, leaves, or feathers.
- Use photos that have been emailed to you.

Be sure you have the right to use the photos or images you choose. Sometimes a company will license an image to you for a small fee. Get permission from the photographer, artist, or designer to use a photograph, drawing, or fabric design. (Louise James received permission from the photographer to use the photos she incorporated in her quilt *Foraging for Mushrooms* on page 47.) A safe bet is to use your own photos—you hold the copyright on those!

Foraging for Mushrooms, 37½″ × 37½″. Border blocks pieced and contributed by the group. Designed and assembled by Louise James, 2005. Machine quilted by Barbara Dau. Photos by Eileen Seto, Wheaton, IL (used with permission).

Visit to the Tulip Fields, 45″ × 45″.
Blocks contributed by the group. Designed
and assembled by Leslie Rommann, 2005.
Machine quilted by Arlene Anderson.

Family Airfare, 52″ × 59″.
Blocks contributed by the group.
Designed and assembled by Barb
Higbee-Price, 2005. Machine quilted
by Stacie Johnson and Debbie Webster.

Pack Your Bags, 45″ × 43″.
Blocks contributed by the group.
Designed, assembled, and machine
quilted by Susie Kincy, 2005.

Love You, Tyler: 1990–2005, 42″ × 42″.
Blocks contributed by the group. Designed and
assembled by Annette Barca, 2005. Machine
quilted by Barbara Dau.

Russian Meditation (triptych), 32″ × 32″ (open). Blocks contributed by the group. Designed, assembled, and quilted by Anastasia Riordan, 2005.

Russian Meditation (triptych), 16″ × 32″ (closed).

Chapter 7

Embellishment and **Embroidery**

As you've probably noticed, many of the quilts in this book—whether my quilts or quilts originating with and owned by others in our exchange group—feature machine embroidery and other forms of embellishment. This is no accident! I *love* threads, yarns, ribbons, tassels, beads, buttons, charms, and other trinkets, and I *love* what they can do to enhance a quilt. (Obviously, my group-mates agree!)

Embroidery and embellishment can play many roles in your quilt's design. You can use these design elements to do the following:

- Add drama

- Introduce whimsy

- Emphasize the theme

- Focus attention on a particular area of the quilt

- Create filler strips or blocks to balance the quilt's setting

- Even cover up— dare I say it?—mistake!

On the following pages are a few examples of embellishing techniques you might try.

COUCHING

In couching, decorative threads or trims are layered over the quilt surface and stitched in place using a zigzag, serpentine, or other decorative stitch and the appropriate foot attachment on your sewing machine. You can couch with thread that matches the color of the trim, or use a different color or texture (e.g., metallic thread) for contrast. You can even leave the ends to dangle free over the edge of the quilt, as I did in *Zulu Love Letter* (see detail below right).

Think ribbons, yarns, threads, tassels, strips of fabric (flat, twisted, or braided), cording, rickrack, lace, and other decorative trims. All are wonderful candidates for couching.

Couching with a fancy trim foot

Couching with a braiding foot

Couching with a narrow braid cord foot

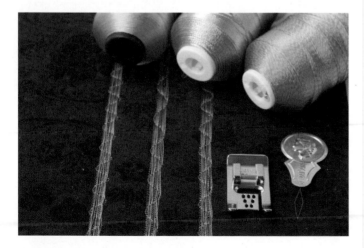

Couching with a 7-hole cording foot

I left the ends of my couched fibers to dangle free at the bottom of *Zulu Love Letter*. For a full view of this quilt, see page 56.

RAW-EDGE AND THREE-DIMENSIONAL APPLIQUÉ

The sky is the limit with raw-edge appliqué! Simply apply fusible web to the fabric of choice, cut out the desired shapes, and follow the manufacturer's instructions to adhere the shapes to the quilt surface. Finish by top stitching the edges with decorative threads and stitchery.

Don't limit yourself to cotton fabric. Try silks, lamé (both cotton and metallic), wool, and organza. Use a Teflon pressing cloth for delicate fabrics; you'll protect your iron from any stray fusible as well.

Another raw-edged alternative is to create three-dimensional appliqués. Fuse two pieces of fabric right sides together and cut out the desired shape, finishing the edges with a satin or other decorative stitch. Rather than stitching down the edges, attach the appliqué to the quilt surface by stitching down the center with decorative thread.

Raw-edge appliqué can add visual interest to the quilt surface.

Carla Zimmermann used dimensional leaf appliqués to bring additional color and texture to *Elf Shadows Guarding the Forest Floor*. For a full view of this quilt, see page 60.

BEADS, BUTTONS, AND OTHER TRINKETS

Where to begin? Besides the "usual" buttons and beads, you can add just about any small three-dimensional goody to your quilt. Sequins, buckles, charms, tiny seashells, washers, "gems and jewels" from costume jewelry—all are fair game in the hands of an inventive embellisher! Take a close look at John James's quilt *The 12th Man* (page 62). He's affixed two dozen collector pins to this ode to his beloved Seattle Seahawks.

You can use any number of techniques to attach interesting items to your quilt. You can stitch, tie, glue, bead, or button them on, or secure them with patches of see-through organza or vinyl. Your only limit is your imagination.

Anastasia Riordan made creative use of embellishment by using hinges to connect the three panels of her triptych *Russian Meditation*. For a full view of this quilt, see page 50.

Tasteful tacking

Instead of using thread to attach raw-edge or dimensional appliqués to the quilt surface, tack them in the center with buttons or beads.

MACHINE EMBROIDERY

Machine embroidery is one of my favorite techniques for embellishment. With the exception of *Where's George?* (page 43), my Photo-Exchange Quilt, I've used it in every quilt I made for this book. If you've never tried it before, an exchange quilt is the perfect canvas to give it a try.

You can incorporate machine embroidery into pieced blocks, in place of a plain fabric square, as I did in *International* (page 15).

You can use it to create unique filler strips, such as the ones I incorporated into the rows of *Inside My Garden Gate*.

You can use it to reinforce the theme of the quilt, as demonstrated by Susie Kincy in the borders of her beautiful quilt *A Passion for Paisley* (page 39).

However you choose to introduce machine embroidery into your work, here are some tips to help you get started:

■ Prewash the fabric you plan to use as the background for the embroidery designs.

■ Begin with a fresh, new needle, and change it during the process if the point becomes dull. Some embroidery designs have in excess of 10,000 stitches. A dull needle can distort the design.

■ Outfit your machine with an embroidery-foot attachment.

Use an embroidery foot to create beautiful machine embroidery.

■ Prewind several bobbins with polyester, rayon, or cotton bobbin-fill thread, such as Robison-Anton polyfilament bobbin thread, or purchase prewound bobbins, such as those manufactured by Robison-Anton. Bobbin thread in white, black, or to match the background fabric are all good choices, but you may prefer to change the bobbin thread as the color of the top thread changes, especially if the embroidery is an appliqué you'll see from both sides.

■ Select a fabric stabilizer to use under the fabric. There are many different types of stabilizers available; whichever you choose, read the manufacturer's instructions *carefully*. I prefer a tear-away stabilizer such as

Inspira Tear-Away Stabilizer or Sulky of America's Tear Easy (medium weight) when I machine embroider on 100% cotton fabric. Sometimes a liquid stabilizer works well with a lightweight or light-colored fabric. If the fabric is prone to puckering, try a water- or heat-soluble stabilizer.

- A hoop keeps the fabric from shifting as you embroider the designs. If possible, place the fabric in the hoop so it is on the straight of grain, pleat- and pucker-free, and taut but not pulled too tightly.

- If the block or the section of the quilt you are working on is too small for the hoop, stitch a piece of waste fabric to the edges. Remove it when you have completed the embroidery.

- Stitch a test of the desired embroidery design using the fabric, threads, and stabilizer you plan to use for the project. You will be able to tell whether the thread tension is correct, whether the thread coverage is sufficient, and how the embroidered design will look on the background fabric you've chosen so you can make any necessary adjustments. If you wish, you can incorporate your test design into your label or quilt backing.

 Not enough blocks?
Fill in with embroidery blocks that coordinate with your theme.

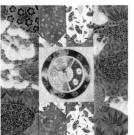

Kimono Garden, 23″ × 32″. **Blocks contributed by the group. Designed, assembled, and machine quilted by Susie Kincy, 2005.**

Embellishment Exchange

Zulu Love Letter, 21″ × 31″. Designed and assembled by M'Liss Rae Hawley, 2005.

This exchange presents a perfect opportunity to learn and practice a variety of the exciting embellishment techniques introduced in the previous chapter. Embellishment options include—but are not limited to—embroidery, couching, decorative machine stitching, raw-edge appliqué, buttons, beads, charms, and other trinkets. See Embellishment and Embroidery, pages 50–55 for ideas and examples.

The quilt consists of four vertical rows: 3˝ × 24˝, 4˝ × 24˝, 3˝ × 24˝, and 4˝ × 24˝ (finished). These rows are the canvas for the group members to embellish. You may choose to use plain (unpieced) strips of focus or theme fabric, pieced and/or embroidered blocks, or a combination of the two. If you choose pieced blocks, you will need eight 3˝ (finished) blocks for each 3˝-wide row and six 4˝ (finished) blocks for each 4˝-wide row.

There are a number of options for orchestrating this exchange:

- You may have the members do just the embellishment.

- You may have the members make the pieced blocks as well.

- You may send the quilt out in strips and assemble them yourself when they are returned.

- You may send the quilt top already assembled, ready for embellishment. (If the quilt is also layered and basted, the embellishment can serve as some— or all—of the quilting.)

Of course, you are always welcome to layer additional embellishment when the quilt or its component parts come back to you!

I selected fabrics from my collection of African textiles and a whimsical embroidery collection featuring animals and symbols of Africa. I combined these with the Pinwheel block, which I used in the alternating rows in my quilt. This block gives the illusion of motion and suggests a youthful, light-hearted attitude. The alternating fabric stripes continue the playful theme and are a wonderful foundation for embellishment.

Note: Materials and cutting specifications listed are for the unpieced blocks and rows, borders, batting, backing, and binding. Materials for individual blocks will depend upon the selection made, and can be found in the Block Pool beginning on page 76. The quilt shown features the 4˝ Pinwheel (page 86) block. Refer to the assembly diagram on page 58 as needed.

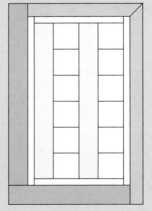

Finished quilt size: 21˝ x 31˝

ZULU LOVE LETTERS (iNewadi)

Zulu maidens weave messages in beads, called "love letters," to be given to their lovers as symbols of affection. My quilt *Zulu Love Letter* is designed around one of these beaded pins. Each color in the pin has a symbolic meaning or message.

White: This color represents purity, vision, and love itself.

Black: "I have turned pitch black as the rafters of the hut because I miss you so."

Blue: "If I were a dove, I would fly to your home and pick up food at your door."

Yellow: "I shall never eat if we marry since you own no beast you can slaughter."

Pink: "You should work harder to get lobola, not gamble and waste your money."

Green: "I have become thin like the sweet cane in a damp field, and green as the first shoots of trees because of my love for you."

Red: "My heart bleeds and is full of love."

This pin was purchased in Africa and given to me by Robyn, one of our former exchange students, who now lives in London. We have stayed in touch all these years!

MATERIALS

All yardage is based on fabric that is 40˝ wide after laundering.

¼ yard for the unpieced blocks

⅓ yard for the unpieced rows

¼ yard for the inner border

⅓ yard *each* of 2 fabrics for the outer border

½ yard for the binding

1 yard for the backing

29˝ × 39˝ piece of batting

CUTTING

Cut all strips across the fabric width.

From the unpieced block fabric:
Cut 1 strip, 4½˝ × 40˝; crosscut 6 squares, 4½˝ × 4½˝.*

From the unpieced row fabric:
Cut 2 strips, 3½˝ × 24½˝.

From the inner border fabric:
Cut 2 strips, 1˝ × 14½˝.

Cut 2 strips, 1˝ × 25½˝.

From outer border fabric 1 (mitered corner):
Cut 1 strip, 3½˝ × 21˝, for the top border.

Cut 1 strip, 3½˝ × 36½˝, for the right side border.

From outer border fabric 2:
Cut 1 strip, 3½˝ × 28½˝, for the left side border.

Cut 1 strip, 3½˝ × 18½˝, for the bottom border.

From the binding fabric:
Cut 4 strips, 3˝ × 40˝.

If you plan to embroider these squares as I did in Zulu Love Letter, cut them slightly oversized and trim when the embroidery is complete.

QUILT ASSEMBLY

1. Sew three 4½˝ pieced blocks and three 4½˝ squares together to make a row, alternating them as shown. Press. Make 1 of each.

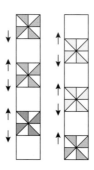

Make 1 each.

2. Refer to the assembly diagram. Arrange the 2 rows from Step 1 and the two 3½˝ × 24½˝ strips, alternating them as shown. Sew the rows and strips together. Press.

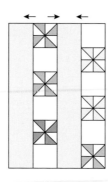

Assembly diagram

3. Refer to Squared Borders (page 68). Sew a 1˝ × 14½˝ inner border strip to the top and bottom of the quilt. Press the seams toward the border. Sew 1˝ × 25½˝ inner borders to the sides. Press.

4. Sew the 3½˝ × 21˝ outer border fabric 1 strip to the top of the quilt, aligning one end of the border strip with the left edge of the quilt. The excess border length will extend beyond the right side of the quilt. Stop sewing approximately ¼˝ from the edge of the quilt and take a back-stitch. Press toward the outer border.

5. Refer to Mitered Borders, Steps 2–4 (page 69), to center and sew the 3½˝ × 36½˝ outer border fabric 1 strip to the right edge of the quilt. Start with a backstitch ¼˝ from the top edge of the quilt and stop approximately 3˝ from the bottom edge of the quilt, as shown. Refer to Mitered Borders, Steps 6–10 (pages 69–70), to miter the upper right corner. Press toward the outer border.

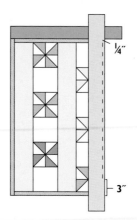

6. Refer to Squared Borders (page 68). Sew the 3½″ × 28½″ outer border fabric 2 strip to the left side of the quilt. Press the seam toward the outer border. Sew the 3½″ × 18½″ outer border fabric 2 strip to the bottom of the quilt. Complete the seam between the bottom and right side borders as shown. Press.

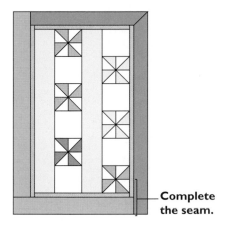

Complete the seam.

FINISHING

Refer to Preparing Your Quilt for Quilting (page 70), Quilting (page 71), and Finishing Your Quilt (page 72).

1. Layer the quilt top, batting, and backing; baste.

2. Hand or machine quilt as desired.

3. Use the 3″-wide strips to bind the edges of the quilt.

4. Add a hanging sleeve and label if desired.

Alternate Quilt

I alternated pieced and unpieced rows in my quilt *Zulu Love Letter* (page 56). If you prefer to substitute unpieced rows for the 2 pieced rows, cut two 4½″ × 24½″ strips from a second row fabric (⅜ yard). Follow Quilt Assembly, Steps 2–5 (page 58), substituting the 4½″ strips for the pieced rows.

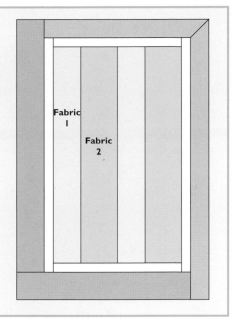

Elf Shadows Guarding the Forest Floor, 25″ × 35″.
Blocks contributed by the group. Designed and assembled by Carla
Zimmermann, 2005. Machine quilted by Cheryl Gilman.

Bob's Paperbark Maple in the Fall, 31˝ × 21˝.
Blocks contributed by the group. Designed, assembled,
and machine quilted by Annette Barca, 2005.

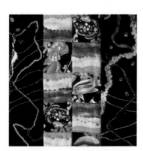

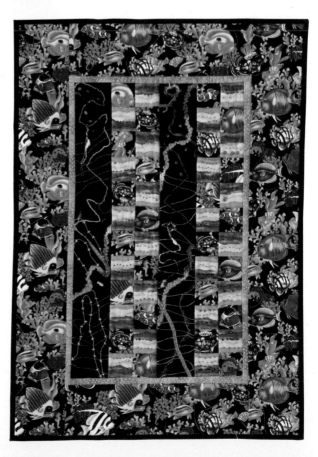

Caribbean Rush Hour, 24˝ × 34˝.
Blocks contributed by the group.
Designed, assembled, and machine
quilted by Marie Miller, 2005.

The 12th Man, 32″ × 22″. Blocks contributed by the group. Designed and assembled by John James, 2005. Machine quilted by Barbara Dau.

My Silk Garden, 21″ × 31″.
Embellishment contributed by the group. Designed and assembled by Barb Higbee-Price, 2005. Machine quilted by Stacie Johnson and Debbie Webster.

Embellished Pillow

All Dressed Up and Nowhere to Go: Kimono Art Pillows 1 & 2.
Designed, embellished, assembled, and machine quilted by M'Liss Rae Hawley, 2005.

Finished pillow sizes: 18″ × 18″

The construction of the Embellished Pillow is similar to that of the small embellished quilt. The four vertical rows measure 3″ × 14″, 4″ × 14″, 3″ × 14″, and 4″ × 14″ (finished). Conduct this exchange just as you would the Embellished Quilt exchange (page 56).

MATERIALS

All yardage is based on fabric that is 40″ wide after laundering.

1 strip *each*, 3½″ × 14½″, from 2 different fabrics for the rows*

1 strip *each*, 4½″ × 14½″, from 2 different fabrics for the rows

¼ yard for the border

½ yard for the backing

18″ × 18″ pillow form

*I used 1″ Checkerboard squares to create these strips in Kimono Art Pillow 2.

CUTTING

Cut all strips across the fabric width.

From the border fabric:
Cut 2 strips, 2½″ × 14½″.

Cut 2 strips, 2½″ × 18½″.

From the backing fabric:
Cut 2 pieces, 18½″ × 12½″.

PILLOW ASSEMBLY

1. Refer to the assembly diagram. Alternate the $3\frac{1}{2}'' \times 14\frac{1}{2}''$ strips and the $4\frac{1}{2}'' \times 14\frac{1}{2}''$ strips, as shown. Sew the strips together. Press.

2. Refer to Squared Borders (page 68). Sew a $2\frac{1}{2}''$-wide border strip to the top and bottom of the quilt. Press. Repeat to sew $2\frac{1}{2}''$-wide borders to the sides. Press.

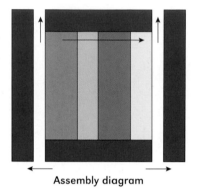

Assembly diagram

3. Fold under a $\frac{1}{4}''$ hem along one $18\frac{1}{2}''$ edge of each $18\frac{1}{2}'' \times 12\frac{1}{2}''$ backing piece. Press. Fold under another $\frac{1}{4}''$. Press and stitch along the folded edge.

4. With right sides up, place one backing piece over the other so the hemmed edges overlap, making the backing piece the same size as the pillow top. Baste the backing pieces together at the top and bottom where they overlap.

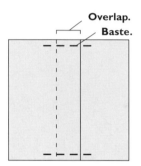

Overlap.
Baste.

Quilt it!

If you wish, you can layer and quilt the pillow top before assembling it into a pillow. You'll need a $22'' \times 22''$ square each of batting and lining fabric. Refer to Preparing Your Quilt for Quilting (page 70) and Quilting (page 71) for guidance as needed. Trim the batting and lining even with the pillow top after quilting.

5. With right sides together, align and pin the pillow top to the backing. Sew around the outside edges with a $\frac{1}{4}''$-wide seam. Remove the basting, trim the corners, and turn the pillow cover right side out. Press before inserting the pillow form.

Bowties for Bowser (pillow), 18" × 18".
Blocks contributed by the group. Designed, assembled, and machine quilted by Leslie Rommann, 2005.

Bob's Paperbark Maple Pillow, 18" × 18".
Designed, assembled, and machine quilted by Annette Barca, 2005.

Chapter 9

Getting Down to Basics

ROTARY CUTTING

Almost all the pieces for the blocks and quilts in this book can be cut with a rotary cutter. It is essential that you square the edges of your fabrics before you rotary cut them into strips and pieces. The edges of the fabric must be straight for the resulting pieces to be straight, and you don't want to waste time—or precious fabric!—by having to stop and recut. Make sure the fabric is pressed and that you fold it carefully before you begin cutting.

Note: Cutting instructions are for right-handers. Reverse if you are left-handed.

1. Fold the fabric from selvage to selvage. Hold the fabric in the air and study the drape. Disregard the cut ends; instead, move the selvages from side to side until the fabric is perfectly flat.

2. Place the fabric on your cutting mat and make a second fold, from selvage edge to folded edge. If you have a large piece of fabric, try to break it down so you can work with a more manageable amount.

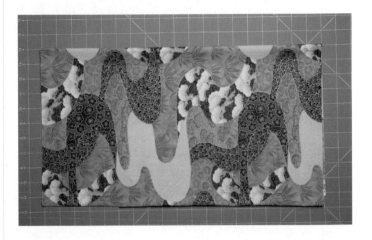

Selvage gone?
You can easily tell the lengthwise grain; it's the edge of the fabric that has no stretch.

To square up your fabric:

1. Place the folded fabric on the cutting mat with the folded edge facing you. Position your ruler on the right edge of the fabric so it is perpendicular to the fold.

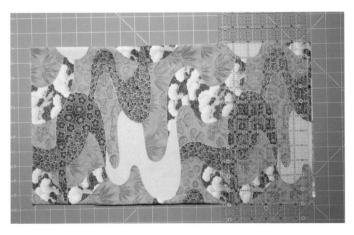

2. Trim a narrow strip from the edge of the fabric to square it up. Rotate the fabric (or the mat), and repeat to trim the opposite edge.

CUTTING STRIPS AND PIECES

Use your ruler, not the markings on the mat, to measure and cut strips and pieces. I use the grid on my mat for aligning the fabric and for taking general measurements, not for making precise measurements.

1. Working with the squared left edge of the fabric, use your ruler to measure and cut a strip of the desired width. Repeat to cut the required number of strips. You may want to square up the edge of the fabric after every few cuts.

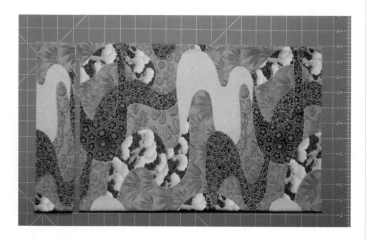

2. Cut the strip into squares or other smaller segments as directed in the project instructions.

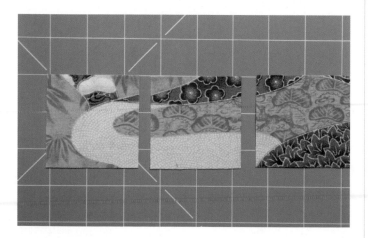

PIECING AND PRESSING

Unless otherwise noted, you'll be using a ¼˝ seam allowance for piecing the blocks and quilts in this book. It's always a good idea to stitch a test piece to check that your ¼˝ seam is accurate before beginning to sew.

The construction process is simple: you'll sew pieces into units, units into rows or sections, and rows or sections together to complete the block or the quilt. The project instructions will tell you which way to press the seams, either in the step itself or with arrows in the accompanying diagrams.

For the blocks, or when in doubt, follow these general guidelines:

- Press lightly in a lifting-and-lowering motion. Dragging the iron across the fabric can distort the individual pieces and finished blocks.

- Press toward the darker fabric when possible.

- Press in opposite directions from row to row. This helps your seams match evenly and lie flat.

FLIP AND SEW

You'll love this quick and easy piecing method! Using only squares and rectangles, you'll achieve perfect little triangles on such blocks as Bowtie (page 78), Flying Geese (page 80), Honeycomb (page 82), Nine-Patch Embroidery (page 84), and Whidbey Star (page 91).

1. Use a ruler and marking tool to draw a diagonal line from corner to corner on the wrong side of each small square, as indicated in the block diagram for the block you are making.

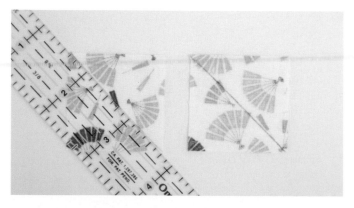

2. With raw edges aligned, place the small marked square right sides together with the larger square or rectangle, as indicated in the block diagram. Sew directly on the diagonal line.

3. Cut away the excess fabric, leaving a ¼″-wide seam allowance. Press the seams toward the small square.

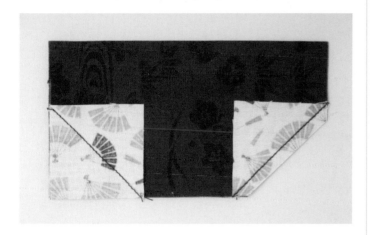

4. Repeat Steps 2 and 3 to add additional squares as needed.

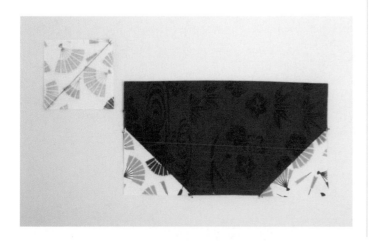

MAKING BIAS STRIPS

Fabric strips cut on the bias have the stretch necessary for making graceful curves. You can use this method to make the stem on the Autumn Leaf block (page 77) and the handle on the Party Basket block (page 85). The block instructions tell you how wide to cut the strips.

1. Use your rotary cutter to cut a strip in the desired width across the bias of the fabric.

2. Fold the strip in half lengthwise, wrong sides together, and sew along the length with a scant ¼″-wide seam. Center the seam on the back of the strip—bias presser bars help here—and press.

3. As you appliqué, tuck the raw edges inside the strip at each end to achieve the desired length.

ASSEMBLING THE QUILT

With the exception of the medallion quilts set on point, all the quilts in this book are sewn together in an arrangement called the straight set. The blocks are arranged in horizontal and/or vertical rows, with the block edges parallel to the sides of the quilt. The blocks are sewn together with ¼″ seams to create the rows. The project instructions advise you which way to press the seams, either in the step itself or with arrows in the accompanying diagrams. Usually seams are pressed in opposite directions from row to row. Then the rows are sewn together and the seams pressed, most often in one direction.

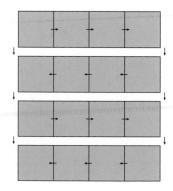

Straight set
Arrows indicate pressing direction.

ADDING BORDERS

Most quilts in this book (including all the project quilts) feature either squared borders or mitered borders.

Squared Borders

Squared borders are the easiest of all borders to sew. Add the top and bottom borders first and then the side borders.

1. Measure the quilt top through the center from side to side, and cut 2 border strips to this measurement. These will be the top and bottom borders.

2. Place pins at the center point of the top and bottom of the quilt top, as well as at the center point of each border strip. Pin the borders to the quilt top, matching the ends and center points. Use additional pins as needed, easing or gently stretching the border to fit.

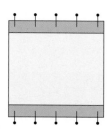

3. Sew the borders to the quilt with a ¼″ seam. Press as instructed—usually toward the border. If the quilt top is slightly longer than the border, stitch with the quilt top on the bottom, closest to the feed dogs. If the reverse is true, stitch with the border on the bottom. The motion of the feed dogs will help ease in the extra length.

4. Measure the quilt top from top to bottom, including the borders you've just sewn, and cut 2 border strips to this measurement. These will be the side borders. Repeat Steps 2 and 3 to pin, sew, and press the borders.

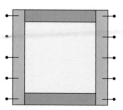

Mitered Borders

Mitered borders require a bit more time and fabric but create a clean picture frame effect.

1. Measure the finished quilt top through the center from top to bottom. Add 2 times the width of the border, plus 5″ for insurance. Cut 2 borders to this measurement; these will be the *side* borders. Measure the finished quilt top through the center from side to side, adding 2 times the width of the border plus 5″, to cut the *top and bottom* borders.

2. Place a pin to mark the center of one side of the quilt top. Place a pin at the center point of the long edge of one of the side border strips. Measure and pin-mark half the length of the quilt top on both sides of the center pin on this border strip.

3. Pin the border to the side of the quilt, matching center point to center point. Match the quilt length, marked by the pins on the border strip, to the edges of the quilt top. The excess border length will extend beyond each end of the quilt.

4. Stitch the border strip to the side of the quilt; start and stop stitching ¼″ from the edge of the quilt with a backstitch. Press the seams toward the borders.

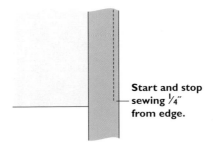

Start and stop sewing ¼″ from edge.

Note: For the Embellishment Exchange project or the Attic Window block, the border strips will extend beyond the end of the quilt only at the corner you are mitering. The other end of the border strip will align with the edge of the quilt. Stop stitching and take a backstitch ¼″ from the edge of the quilt where the miter will be.

5. Repeat Steps 2–4 to pin and sew the remaining side border and the top and bottom borders to the quilt. Press.

6. To create the miter, place one corner of the quilt or block right side up on your ironing board. Place the excess "tail" of one border strip on top of the adjacent border. Fold the top border strip under at a 45° angle so it aligns with the edge of the border underneath, as shown. Press the fold lightly.

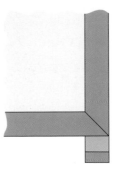

7. Use a ruler or right-angle triangle to be certain the angle is correct and the corner is square. Press again, firmly.

8. Fold the quilt top or block diagonally, right sides together, aligning the 45° pressing marks and the long edges of the border strips. Place pins near the pressed fold to secure the corners of the border strips for sewing.

9. Beginning with a backstitch at the border seam at the inside corner of the miter, carefully stitch toward the outside edge along the fold. Finish with a backstitch.

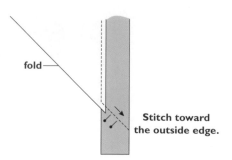

fold

Stitch toward the outside edge.

10. Trim the excess border fabric, leaving a ¼″-wide seam allowance, and press the seam open.

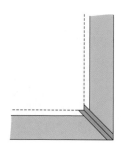

PREPARING YOUR QUILT FOR QUILTING

As with every step of quiltmaking, this step is important. Don't skimp here! Take time to layer properly and baste sufficiently. The results—a nice, flat quilt, free from puckers and bumps—will make you proud.

Batting and Backing

Choice of batting is a personal decision, but you'll want to consider the method (and amount) of quilting you plan to do, as well as the quilt's end use. Since I prefer machine quilting, I usually use cotton batting in a heavier weight for bed quilts and wallhangings and a lighter weight for clothing. You'll probably want to stick with lightweight batting for hand quilting. Polyester batting is a good choice for tied quilts.

No matter which type of batting you choose, cut the batting approximately 4″ larger than the quilt top on all sides.

As with the batting, you'll want the quilt backing to be approximately 4″ larger than the quilt top on all sides. You'll sometimes need to piece the fabric to have a large enough backing piece. Prewash the backing fabric and remove the selvages first.

Layering and Basting

Unlike many machine quilters, I prefer to hand baste with thread rather than pin baste. That allows me to machine quilt without having to stop to remove pins.

1. Carefully press the quilt top from the back to set the seams, and then press from the front. Press the backing. If you wish, use spray starch or sizing.

2. Spread the backing wrong side up on a clean, flat surface, and secure it with masking tape. The fabric should be taut but not stretched. Center the batting over the backing, and secure. Finally, center the quilt top over the batting.

3. Thread a long needle with light-colored thread. Beginning in the center of the quilt, stitch a 4″ grid of horizontal and vertical lines.

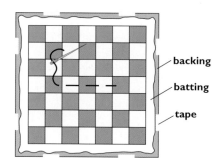

backing

batting

tape

4. When you've finished basting, remove the tape and get ready to quilt!

QUILTING

A quilt becomes a quilt when it includes three layers—a top, a filler layer or batting, and a backing—all attached with stitching of some type to hold the layers together. (That means that to call your project a quilt, you need to finish it!) Some quilters create that stitching by hand, others by machine. My quilts in this book—as well as almost all the quilts made by my wonderful group of quilters—are machine quilted.

Each step of the quiltmaking process is exciting and fun to me, including the machine quilting. I love the idea of adding yet another level of creativity to my quilts. Machine quilting my own tops gives me flexibility in making those design decisions, and I do my own quilting whenever I can. Because of time constraints, however, I find I must now have many of my quilt tops professionally machine quilted. If you have stacks of quilt tops waiting to be quilted, you might want to consider that option, too.

Machine quilting is an art form, so there is a learning curve involved. Practice is the best way to learn and master this skill. Here are some guidelines to get you started.

Dual-Feed Foot

The dual-feed foot is designed to hold and feed the three layers of your quilt evenly as you stitch. Use this foot to stitch single or parallel lines and grids—whether vertical, horizontal, or diagonal. You can also use this foot when you use certain decorative stitches and embellishing techniques, such as couching (page 52), to machine quilt.

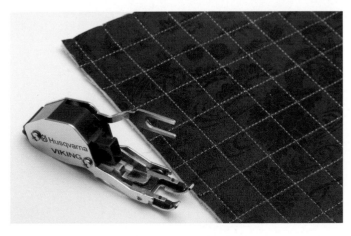

Use a dual-feed foot for straight-line quilting.

Open-Toe Stippling Foot

Also called a darning foot, the open-toe stippling foot allows you to quilt in all directions: you are the guide! Use this foot for stipple quilting, meandering, and other free-motion techniques. I like to stipple quilt around machine-embroidered motifs. This causes the embroidered design to pop out and become a focal point.

Use an open-toe foot for free-motion quilting.

You will need to drop the feed dogs on your sewing machine when you use the open-toe stippling foot. You may also need to set the presser foot pressure to the darning position so you can move the quilt at a smooth pace for consistent stitches. Some machines have a built-in stipple stitch, which is a wonderful way to achieve this beautiful surface texture.

Threads

I consider quilting thread to be a design element, not just the means to hold the three layers of my quilt together. I also believe that variety in thread adds visual interest and showcases the individuality of the quilter. For these reasons, I frequently use a mix of threads in my quilts. When choosing thread, I consider thread color, texture, and weight and where I plan to use the thread.

Typical thread choices for machine quilting include rayon (35- and 40-weight), cotton, polyester, and monofilament. I use lots of variegated and metallic threads, and novelty threads such as Twister Tweeds, Swirling Sensation, and Moon Glow. The latter are manufactured by Robison-Anton. (See Resources, page 94.)

Design

Let your imagination be your guide in choosing quilting motifs for your quilts. Design sources are everywhere! Look carefully at quilts in museums, shows, books, and magazines; at books of quilting patterns; and at quilting stencils. Observe patterns in other areas of your life—particularly patterns in nature.

In addition to the basics (in-the-ditch, outline, straight-line, and stipple quilting), try filling in open spaces with loops, curves, clamshells, and waves. Combine straight and curvy lines for variety.

Another option is to let the fabric inspire you and to simply follow a pattern in the fabric with your stitching. Create a garden trellis over a floral fabric, or add detail to a beach with quilted rocks and shells.

Fabric motifs are great inspiration for quilting designs.

FINISHING YOUR QUILT

Your quilt's binding, hanging sleeve, and label are important too, so be sure to give them the same attention you've given to every other step of the process.

Squaring Up

Before adding the binding, you need to trim the excess batting and backing and square up your quilt. Use the seam of the outer border as a guide.

1. Align a ruler with the outer border seam and measure to the edge of the quilt in a number of places. Use the narrowest measurement as a guide for positioning your ruler, and trim the excess batting and backing all around the quilt.

2. Fold the quilt in half lengthwise and crosswise to check that the corners are square and the sides are equal in length. If not, use a large square ruler to correct this, one corner at a time.

Square up the corners.

3. Stabilize the edges of the quilt by stitching around the perimeter with a basting or serpentine stitch. (Do not use a zigzag stitch.)

Serpentine stitch around quilt perimeter.

4. Remove any stray threads or bits of batting from the quilt top, and you are ready to bind your quilt.

Making and Applying Binding

Binding is an important and, sadly, often overlooked step in the quiltmaking process. Many a wonderful quilt is spoiled by a poorly sewn binding. Take your time deciding what fabric you will use, and enjoy the process of stitching it to your quilt. You're coming down the home stretch now!

Typically, I cut binding strips 3″ wide from selvage to selvage across the width of the fabric. I make an exception and cut strips on the bias only when I want to create a special effect with a plaid or striped fabric or when I need to follow a curved or rounded edge.

The following method is the one I use to bind my quilts. It results in a finished edge that is attractive and strong.

1. Cut enough binding strips to go around the perimeter (outside edges) of the quilt plus an extra 10″ for seams and corners. Sew the strips together at right angles, as shown. Trim the excess fabric, leaving a ¼″ seam allowance, and press the seams open.

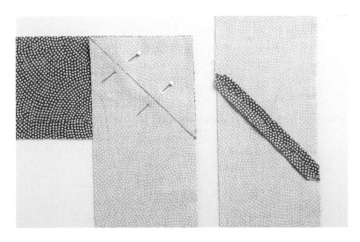

2. Fold the binding in half lengthwise, wrong sides together, and press.

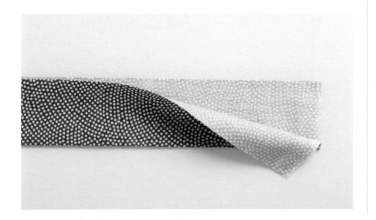

3. Starting 6″ down from the upper right corner and with the raw edges even, lay the binding on the quilt top. Check to see that none of the mitered seams falls on a corner of the quilt. If one does, adjust the starting point. Begin stitching 4″ from the end of the binding, using a ½″ seam allowance.

4. Stitch about 2″, stop, and cut the threads. Remove the quilt from the machine and fold the binding to the back of the quilt. The binding should cover the line of machine stitching on the back. If the binding overlaps the stitching too much, try again, stitching just outside the first line of stitching. If the binding doesn't cover the original line of stitching, stitch just inside the line. Remove the unwanted stitches before you continue.

5. Using the position you determined for stitching in Step 4, resume stitching until you are ½″ from the first corner of the quilt. Stop, backstitch, cut the thread, and remove the quilt from the machine.

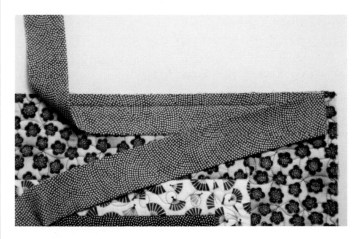

Stop stitching ½″ from corner.

6. Fold the binding up at a 45° angle and then down again, aligning the raw edges of the binding and the quilt to create a mitered corner. Resume stitching, mitering each corner as you come to it.

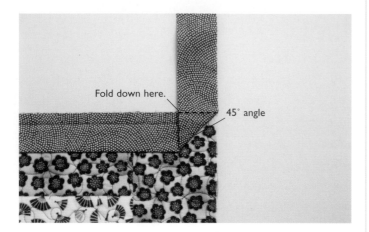

7. Stop stitching about 3″ after you've turned the last corner. Make sure the starting and finishing ends of the binding overlap by at least 4″. Cut the threads and remove the quilt from the machine. Measure a 3″ overlap and trim the excess binding.

8. Lay the quilt right side up. Unfold the unstitched tails, place them right sides together at right angles, and pin. Draw a line from the upper left corner to the lower right corner of the binding, as shown, and stitch on the drawn line.

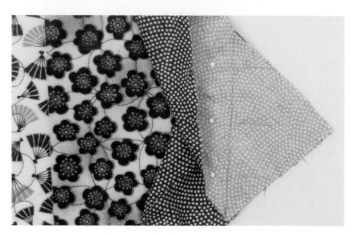

9. Carefully trim the seam allowance to ¼″, and press the seam open. Refold the binding and press. Finish stitching the binding to the quilt.

10. Turn the binding to the back of the quilt, and pin. (I pin approximately 12″ at a time.) Using matching-colored thread, blindstitch the binding to the quilt back, carefully mitering the corners as you approach them. Hand stitch the miters on both sides, as shown.

Making and Adding a Sleeve

If you want to display your quilt on a wall, you need to add a sleeve to protect your work of art from undue strain.

1. Cut an 8½˝-wide strip of fabric 1˝ shorter than the width of the quilt. (If the quilt is wider than 40˝, cut 2 strips and stitch them together end to end.) Fold the short ends under ¼˝, stitch, and press.

2. Fold the sleeve lengthwise, right sides together. Sew the long raw edges, and press. Turn the sleeve right side out, and press again.

3. Match the center point of the top edge of the quilt with the center point of the sleeve. Pin the sleeve to the quilt, right below the binding. Use matching-colored thread to blindstitch the top edge in place.

4. Push the bottom edge of the sleeve up a tiny bit so that when inserted, the hanging rod does not put strain on the quilt. Blindstitch the bottom edge of the sleeve, taking care not to catch the front of the quilt as you stitch.

Creating a Label

I always recommend that you make a label for your quilt. This gives you a place to provide important information about both you and the quilt. I like to make my labels large—about 6˝ × 8˝—so I have plenty of room. You can sew the label to the lower right corner of the quilt back before it is quilted or wait until after the quilt is complete.

I suggest you always include the following information on your label: the name of the quilt; your full name (and business name, if you have one); your city, county, province or state, and country of residence; and the date.

If the quilt was made for a special person, to commemorate a special event, or as part of a series, you may want to include that information as well. You may also choose to note the name of the quilting teacher who inspired you, or tell a special story connected to the quilt.

Use the label to record key information about your quilt.

You can make a simple label by drawing and writing on fabric with permanent fabric markers. (Stabilize the fabric first with freezer paper or interfacing.) For a more elaborate (and fun!) label, try photo-transfer techniques, use the lettering system on your sewing machine, or use an embroidery machine to embellish your label. You may even want to create your own distinctive signature or logo. Include patches, decals, buttons, ribbons, or lace. I often include leftover blocks to tie the quilt top to the back.

Block Pool

The Block Pool is your vehicle to creativity! Use it as a resource to select blocks for your own quilt or for a quilt you are working on for one of your exchange members. Consider it the starting point for your creative group adventure: add fabric, thread, out-of-the-ordinary quilting motifs, and embellishment—then mix in an inventive setting and you are on your way.

There are 30 blocks or block units in the Block Pool, some in multiple sizes. You'll find blocks or units that finish 2″, 3″, 4″, 6″, and 12″, giving you loads of flexibility. To help you out, I've indexed them below according to size.

Don't feel restricted, though, by the blocks you see here. Check your favorite quilt books and magazines for other block options. C&T Publishing's *Quick & Easy Block Tool* is a fabulous source, presenting over 100 blocks in a variety of sizes, all designed for rotary cutting (see Resources, page 94).

Refer to Piecing and Pressing (page 66) for guidance in constructing the blocks and block units.

BLOCK INDEX (BY SIZE):

3″ blocks: Bowtie, Four-Patch, Nine-Patch, Pinwheel, Shoo Fly, Triple Rail

4″ blocks: Bowtie, Broken Dishes, Double Bluff, Four-Patch, Pinwheel, Single Irish Chain, Useless Bay

6″ blocks: Attic Window, Autumn Leaf, Birds in the Air, Broken Dishes, Double Bluff, Kaleidoscope, Log Cabin, Ohio Star, Party Basket, Pinwheel, Prairie Queen, Sawtooth Star, Shoo Fly, Single Irish Chain, Useless Bay, Waterwheel, Whirligig

12″ blocks: Autumn Leaf, Nine-Patch Embroidery, Ohio Star, Pink Magnolia, Sister's Choice, Tumbling Star, Waterwheel, Whidbey Star

Odd-sized blocks and units (to use in larger blocks and as borders or fillers): Checkerboard, Flying Geese, Half-Square Triangle, Honeycomb

Blocks and units in multiple sizes: Autumn Leaf, Bowtie, Broken Dishes, Double Bluff, Four-Patch, Honeycomb, Ohio Star, Pinwheel, Shoo Fly, Single Irish Chain, Useless Bay, Waterwheel

In cutting instructions and diagrams, letters (e.g., A, B) represent shapes and numbers (e.g., 1, 2) represent fabrics.

Unless noted otherwise, cutting instructions yield one block. For blocks given in multiple sizes, construction is the same, regardless of the block size. All blocks pieced by M'Liss Rae Hawley, Vicki DeGraaf, Peggy Johnson, and Susie Kincy.

Do your quilts go together perfectly?

Have you stopped and measured your blocks recently? Accuracy really matters! For a group quilt to work, each block must match the required measurement.

6"

6" & 12"

Attic **Window**

Refer to Mitered Borders, (page 69), to complete this block using the 2″ × 9″ strips as the left side and bottom borders.

Cutting

6″ Block

From *each* of Fabric 1 and Fabric 2:
Cut 1 strip, 2″ × 9″ (A1 and A2).

From Fabric 3:
Cut 1 square, 5″ × 5″ (B).

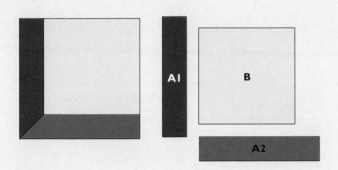

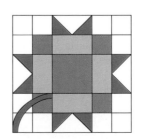

Plan ahead!

If you plan to embroider B, as I have in the quilts on pages 15, 20, and 33, I recommend you cut the square oversize, and then trim it to 5″ × 5″ when you've completed the embroidery. See Machine Embroidery (page 54) for additional tips and information.

Autumn **Leaf**

The leaf stem (F) is cut from the bias of the fabric. See Making Bias Strips (page 67). Use your preferred method to appliqué the stem to the block.

Cutting

6″ Block

From Fabric 1:
Cut 12 squares, 1½″ × 1½″ (A1).

Cut 1 square, 3¼″ × 3¼″; cut twice diagonally to yield 4 quarter-square triangles (C).

From Fabric 2:
Cut 4 squares, 1⅞″ × 1⅞″; cut each square once diagonally to yield 2 half-square triangles (8 total) (B).

Cut 1 strip, 1¼″ × 5″, from the bias of the fabric (F).

From Fabric 3:
Cut 4 strips, 1½″ × 2½″ (D).

From Fabric 4:
Cut 4 squares, 1½″ × 1½″ (A4).

Cut 1 square, 2½″ × 2½″ (E).

12″ Block

From Fabric 1:
Cut 12 squares, 2½″ × 2½″ (A1).

Cut 1 square, 5¼″ × 5¼″; cut twice diagonally to yield 4 quarter-square triangles (C).

From Fabric 2:
Cut 4 squares, 2⅞″ × 2⅞″, cut each square once diagonally to yield 2 half-square triangles (8 total) (B).

Cut 1 strip, 1½″ × 7½″, from the bias of the fabric (F).

From Fabric 3:
Cut 4 strips, 2½″ × 4½″ (D).

From Fabric 4:
Cut 4 squares, 2½″ × 2½″ (A4).

Cut 1 square, 4½″ × 4½″ (E).

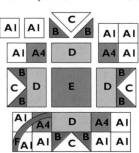

6"

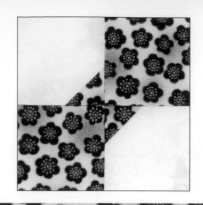

3" & 4"

Birds in the Air

Cutting

6" Block

From Fabric 1:

Cut 2 squares, $2\frac{7}{8}'' \times 2\frac{7}{8}''$; cut each square once diagonally to yield 2 half-square triangles (4 total) (A1). You will have 1 triangle left over.

From Fabric 2:

Cut 3 squares, $2\frac{7}{8}'' \times 2\frac{7}{8}''$; cut each square once diagonally to yield 2 half-square triangles (6 total) (A2).

Cut 1 square, $6\frac{7}{8}'' \times 6\frac{7}{8}''$; cut once diagonally to yield 2 half-square triangles (B). You will have 1 triangle left over.

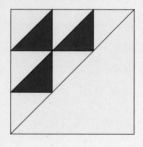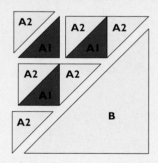

Bowtie

This block is assembled using the Flip and Sew method (page 66).

Cutting

3" Block

From Fabric 1:

Cut 2 squares, $1\frac{1}{4}'' \times 1\frac{1}{4}''$ (A).

Cut 2 squares, $2'' \times 2''$ (B1).

From Fabric 2:

Cut 2 squares, $2'' \times 2''$ (B2).

4" Block

From Fabric 1:

Cut 2 squares, $1\frac{1}{2}'' \times 1\frac{1}{2}''$ (A).

Cut 2 squares, $2\frac{1}{2}'' \times 2\frac{1}{2}''$ (B1).

From Fabric 2:

Cut 2 squares, $2\frac{1}{2}'' \times 2\frac{1}{2}''$ (B2).

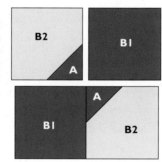

4″ & 6″

1″ squares

Broken Dishes

Cutting

4″ Block

From *each* of Fabrics 1–4: Cut 1 square, 2⅞″ × 2⅞″; cut once diagonally to yield 2 half-square triangles (A1, A2, A3, and A4).

6″ Block

From *each* of Fabrics 1–4: Cut 1 square, 3⅞″ × 3⅞″; cut once diagonally to yield 2 half-square triangles (A1, A2, A3, and A4).

Checkerboard

1″ squares (Unit shown is 4 squares × 3 squares and finishes 4″ × 3″.)

Cutting

4″ × 3″ Unit

From *each* of Fabric 1 and Fabric 2: Cut 6 squares, 1½″ × 1½″ (A1 and A2).

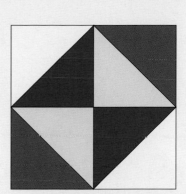

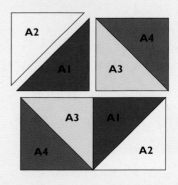

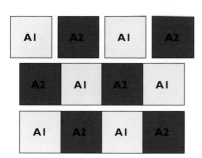

4″ & 6″

2″ × 4″

Double **Bluff**

Cutting

4″ Block

From each of Fabric 1 and Fabric 2:
Cut 1 square, 2⅞″ × 2⅞″; cut once diagonally to yield 2 half-square triangles (A1 and A2).

From Fabric 3:
Cut 2 squares, 2½″ × 2½″ (B).

6″ Block

From each of Fabric 1 and Fabric 2:
Cut 1 square, 3⅞″ × 3⅞″; cut once diagonally to yield 2 half-square triangles (A1 and A2).

From Fabric 3:
Cut 2 squares, 3½″ × 3½″ (B).

Flying **Geese**

This block is assembled using the Flip and Sew method (page 66).

Cutting

2″ × 4″ Unit

From Fabric 1:
Cut 2 squares, 2½″ × 2½″ (A).

From Fabric 2:
Cut 1 rectangle, 2½″ × 4½″ (B).

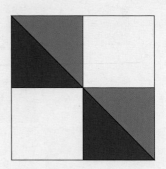

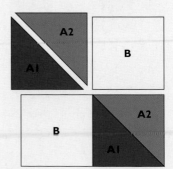

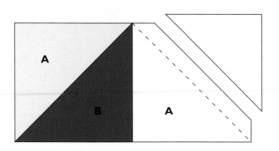

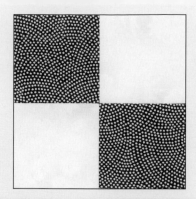

3″ & 4″

2″

Four-Patch

Cutting

3″ Block

From *each* of Fabric 1 and Fabric 2:
Cut 2 squares, 2″ × 2″ (A1 and A2).

4″ Block

From *each* of Fabric 1 and Fabric 2:
Cut 2 squares, 2½″ × 2½″ (A1 and A2).

Half-Square Triangle

Cutting

2″ Block

Makes 2.

From *each* of Fabric 1 and Fabric 2:
Cut 1 square, 2⅞″ × 2⅞″; cut once diagonally to yield 2 half-square triangles (A1 and A2).

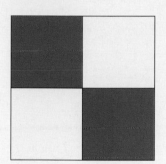

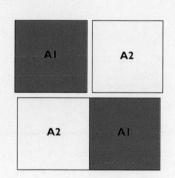

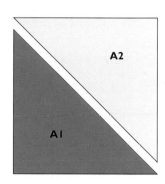

2″x 4″
3″x 6″

6″

Honeycomb

This block is assembled using the Flip and Sew method (page 66).

Cutting

2″ × 4″ Unit

From Fabric 1:
Cut 4 squares, 1½″ × 1½″ (A).

From Fabric 2:
Cut 1 rectangle, 2½″ × 4½″ (B).

3″ × 6″ Unit

From Fabric 1:
Cut 4 squares, 2″ × 2″ (A).

From Fabric 2:
Cut 1 rectangle, 3½″ × 6½″ (B).

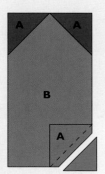

Kaleidoscope

Cutting

6″ Block

From each of Fabric 1 and Fabric 2:
Cut 4 A (A1 and A2).

From Fabric 3:
Cut 4 B.

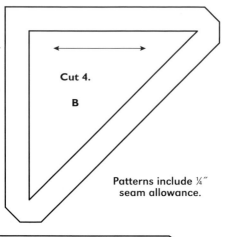

Cut 4.

B

Patterns include ¼″ seam allowance.

Cut 4 *each* from Fabrics 1 & 2.

A
(A1 and A2)

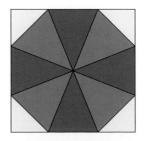
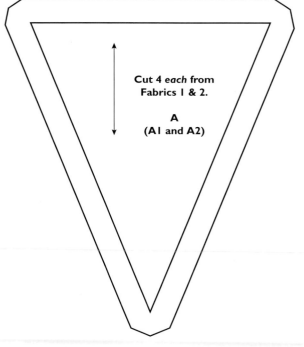
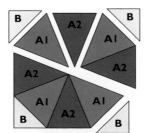

6″

3″

Log **Cabin**

Cutting

6″ Block

From Fabric 1:

Cut 1 square, 2½″ × 2½″ (A).

From Fabric 2:

Cut 1 strip, 1½″ × 2½″ (B).

Cut 1 strip, 1½″ × 4½″ (D2).

From Fabric 3:

Cut 2 strips, 1½″ × 3½″ (C).

From Fabric 4:

Cut 1 strip, 1½″ × 4½″ (D4).

Cut 1 strip, 1½″ × 6½″ (F).

From Fabric 5:

Cut 2 strips, 1½″ × 5½″ (E).

Nine-Patch

Cutting

3″ Block

From Fabric 1:

Cut 5 squares, 1½″ × 1½″ (A1).

From Fabric 2:

Cut 4 squares, 1½″ × 1½″ (A2).

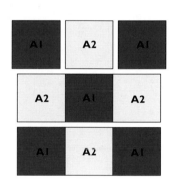

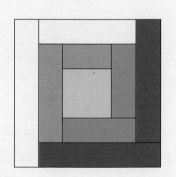

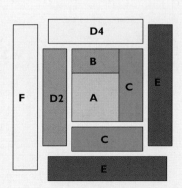

12″

6″ & 12″

Nine-Patch
Embroidery

This block is assembled using the Flip and Sew method (page 66).

Cutting

12″ Block

From Fabric 1:

Cut 10 squares, 2½″ × 2½″ (A1).

Cut 8 squares, 2½″ × 2½″ (B).

From Fabric 2:

Cut 8 squares, 2½″ × 2½″ (A2).

Cut 2 squares, 6½″ × 6½″ (C).

Plan ahead!

If you plan to embroider C, I recommend you cut the square oversize, and then trim it to 6½″ × 6½″ when you've completed the embroidery. See Machine Embroidery (page 54) for additional tips and information.

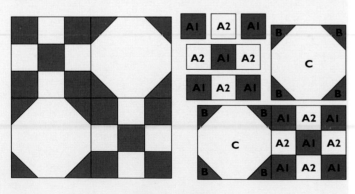

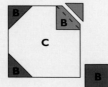

Ohio **Star**

Cutting

6″ Block

From Fabric 1:

Cut 1 square, 3¼″ × 3¼″; cut twice diagonally to yield 4 quarter-square triangles (A1).

Cut 4 squares, 2½″ × 2½″ (B1).

From Fabric 2:

Cut 2 squares, 3¼″ × 3¼″; cut each square twice diagonally to yield 4 quarter-square triangles (8 total) (A2).

From Fabric 3:

Cut 1 square, 3¼″ × 3¼″; cut twice diagonally to yield 4 quarter-square triangles (A3).

From Fabric 4:

Cut 1 square, 2½″ × 2½″ (B4).

12″ Block

From Fabric 1:

Cut 1 square, 5¼″ × 5¼″; cut twice diagonally to yield 4 quarter-square triangles (A1).

Cut 4 squares, 4½″ × 4½″ (B1).

From Fabric 2:

Cut 2 squares, 5¼″ × 5¼″; cut each square twice diagonally to yield 4 quarter-square triangles (8 total) (A2).

From Fabric 3:

Cut 1 square, 5¼″ × 5¼″; cut twice diagonally to yield 4 quarter-square triangles (A3).

From Fabric 4:

Cut 1 square, 4½″ × 4½″ (B4).

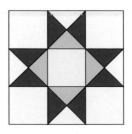

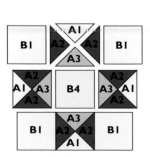

6″

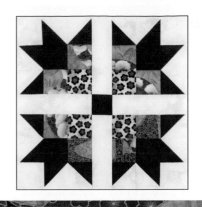

12″

Party **Basket**

The basket handle (D) is cut from the bias of the fabric. See Making Bias Strips (page 67). Use your preferred method to appliqué the handle to the block.

Cutting

6″ Block

From Fabric 1:

Cut 1 square, 4⅞″ × 4⅞; cut once diagonally to yield 2 half-square triangles (A1).

Cut 2 squares, 2½″ × 2½″ (B).

From Fabric 2:

Cut 1 square, 4⅞″ × 4⅞; cut once diagonally to yield 2 half-square triangles (A2). You will have 1 triangle left over.

Cut 1 square, 2⅞″ × 2⅞; cut once diagonally to yield 2 half-square triangles (C).

Cut 1 strip, 1¼″ × 7½″, from the bias of the fabric (D).

Pink **Magnolia**

Cutting

12″ Block

From Fabric 1:

Cut 8 squares, 2¼″ × 2¼″ (A1).

From Fabric 2:

Cut 4 squares, 2¼″ × 2¼″ (A2).

From Fabric 3:

Cut 8 squares, 2⅝″ × 2⅝″; cut each square once diagonally to yield 2 half-square triangles (16 total) (B3).

Cut 4 squares, 2¼″ × 2¼″ (A3).

Cut 1 square, 2″ × 2″ (D).

From Fabric 4:

Cut 8 squares, 2⅝″ × 2⅝″; cut each square once diagonally to yield 2 half-square triangles (16 total) (B4).

Cut 4 squares, 2¼″ × 2¼″ (A4).

Cut 4 strips, 2″ × 5¼″ (C).

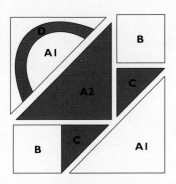

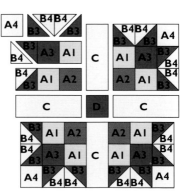

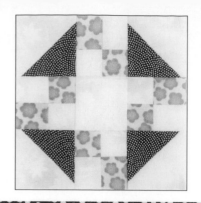

3″, 4″ & 6″

6″

Pinwheel

Cutting

3″ Block

From *each* of Fabric 1 and Fabric 2:

Cut 2 squares, 2⅜″ × 2⅜″; cut each square once diagonally to yield 2 half-square triangles (4 total) (A1 and A2).

4″ Block

From *each* of Fabric 1 and Fabric 2:

Cut 2 squares, 2⅞″ × 2⅞″; cut each square once diagonally to yield 2 half-square triangles (4 total) (A1 and A2).

6″ Block

From *each* of Fabric 1 and Fabric 2:

Cut 2 squares, 3⅞″ × 3⅞″; cut each square once diagonally to yield 2 half-square triangles (4 total) (A1 and A2).

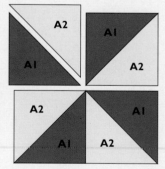

Prairie Queen

Cutting

6″ Block

From Fabric 1:

Cut 2 squares, 2⅞″ × 2⅞″; cut each square once diagonally to yield 2 half-square triangles (4 total) (A1).

Cut 8 squares, 1½″ × 1½″ (B1).

Cut 1 square, 2½″ × 2½″ (C).

From Fabric 2:

Cut 2 squares, 2⅞″ × 2⅞″; cut each square once diagonally to yield 2 half-square triangles (4 total) (A2).

From Fabric 3:

Cut 8 squares, 1½″ × 1½″ (B3).

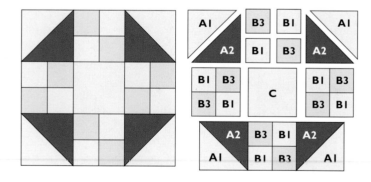

6″

3″ & 6″

Sawtooth **Star**

Cutting

6″ Block

From Fabric 1:

Cut 4 squares, 2⅜″ × 2⅜″; cut each square once diagonally to yield 2 half-square triangles (8 total) (A).

Cut 1 square, 3½″ × 3½″ (D).

From Fabric 2:

Cut 1 square, 4¼″ × 4¼″; cut twice diagonally to yield 4 quarter-square triangles (B).

Cut 4 squares, 2″ × 2″ (C).

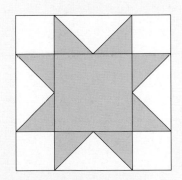

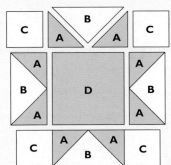

Shoo **Fly**

Cutting

3″ Block

From Fabric 1:

Cut 2 squares, 1⅞″ × 1⅞″; cut each square once diagonally to yield 2 half-square triangles (4 total) (A1).

Cut 4 squares, 1½″ × 1½″ (B1).

From Fabric 2:

Cut 2 squares, 1⅞″ × 1⅞″; cut each square once diagonally to yield 2 half-square triangles (4 total) (A2).

Cut 1 square, 1½″ × 1½″ (B2).

6″ Block

From Fabric 1:

Cut 2 squares, 2⅞″ × 2⅞″; cut each square once diagonally to yield 2 half-square triangles (4 total) (A1).

Cut 4 squares, 2½″ × 2½″ (B1).

From Fabric 2:

Cut 2 squares, 2⅞″ × 2⅞″; cut each square once diagonally to yield 2 half-square triangles (4 total) (A2).

Cut 1 square, 2½″ × 2½″ (B2).

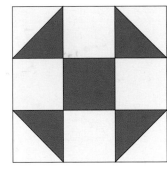

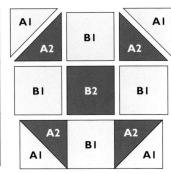

4" & 6"

12"

Single Irish Chain

Cutting

4" Block

From Fabric 1:
Cut 1 square, 2⅞″ × 2⅞″; cut once diagonally to yield 2 half-square triangles (A1).

From Fabric 2:
Cut 1 square, 2⅞″ × 2⅞″; cut once diagonally to yield 2 half-square triangles (A2).

Cut 4 squares, 1½″ × 1½″ (B2).

From Fabric 3
Cut 4 squares, 1½″ × 1½″ (B3).

6" Block

From Fabric 1:
Cut 1 square, 3⅞″ × 3⅞″; cut once diagonally to yield 2 half-square triangles (A1).

From Fabric 2:
Cut 1 square, 3⅞″ × 3⅞″; cut once diagonally to yield 2 half-square triangles (A2).

Cut 4 squares, 2″ × 2″ (B2).

From Fabric 3:
Cut 4 squares, 2″ × 2″ (B3).

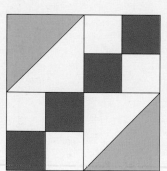

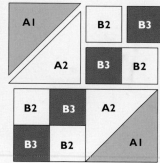

Sister's Choice

Cutting

12" Block

From Fabric 1:
Cut 4 squares, 2⅞″ × 2⅞″ (A1).

Cut 4 squares, 3¼″ × 3¼″; cut each square once diagonally to yield 2 half-square triangles (8 total) (B1).

From Fabric 2:
Cut 4 rectangles, 2⅞″ × 3″ (C2).*

Cut 1 square, 3″ × 3″ (D).

From Fabric 3:
Cut 4 squares, 3¼″ × 3¼″; cut each square once diagonally to yield 2 half-square triangles (8 total) (B3).

From Fabric 4:
Cut 4 squares, 2⅞″ × 2⅞″ (A4).

From Fabric 5:
Cut 4 rectangles, 2⅞″ × 3″ (C5).*

*When piecing, match the 2⅞″ side of the C pieces to the A and B pieces. Match the 3″ side of the C pieces to the D piece.

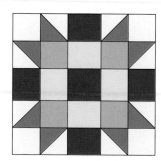

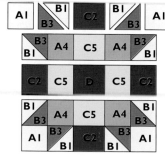

3"

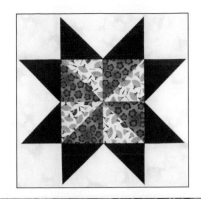

12"

Triple **Rail**

Cutting

3˝ Block

From Fabric 1:

Cut 2 strips, 1½˝ × 3½˝ (A1).

From Fabric 2:

Cut 1 strip, 1½˝ × 3½˝ (A2).

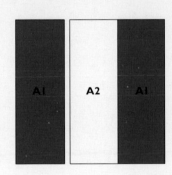

Tumbling **Star**

Cutting

12˝ Block

From *each* of Fabric 1 and Fabric 2:

Cut 2 squares, 3⅞˝ × 3⅞˝; cut each square once diagonally to yield 2 half-square triangles (4 total) (A1 and A2).

From Fabric 3:

Cut 4 squares, 3⅞˝ × 3⅞˝; cut each square once diagonally to yield 2 half-square triangles (8 total) (A3).

From Fabric 4:

Cut 1 square, 7¼˝ × 7¼˝; cut twice diagonally to yield 4 quarter-square triangles (B).

Cut 4 squares, 3½˝ × 3½˝ (C).

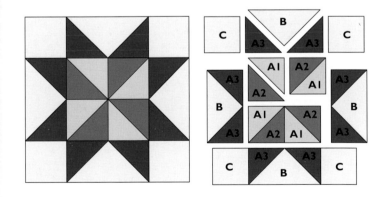

4″ & 6″

6″ & 12″

Useless **Bay**

Cutting

4″ Block

From Fabric 1:

Cut 1 square, 2⅞″ × 2⅞″; cut once diagonally to yield 2 half-square triangles (A1).

From Fabric 2:

Cut 1 square, 2⅞″ × 2⅞″; cut once diagonally to yield 2 half-square triangles (A2).

Cut 4 squares, 1½″ × 1½″ (B2).

From Fabric 3:

Cut 4 squares, 1½″ × 1½″ (B3).

6″ Block

From Fabric 1:

Cut 1 square, 3⅞″ × 3⅞″; cut once diagonally to yield 2 half-square triangles (A1).

From Fabric 2:

Cut 1 square, 3⅞″ × 3⅞″; cut once diagonally to yield 2 half-square triangles (A2).

Cut 4 squares, 2″ × 2″ (B2).

From Fabric 3:

Cut 4 squares, 2″ × 2″ (B3).

Waterwheel

Cutting

6″ Block

From Fabric 1:

Cut 10 squares, 1½″ × 1½″ (A1).

Cut 2 squares, 2⅞″ × 2⅞″; cut each square once diagonally to yield 2 half-square triangles (4 total) (B1).

From Fabric 2:

Cut 10 squares, 1½″ × 1½″ (A2).

From Fabric 3:

Cut 2 squares, 2⅞″ × 2⅞″; cut each square once diagonally to yield 2 half-square triangles (4 total) (B3).

12″ Block

From Fabric 1:

Cut 10 squares, 2½″ × 2½″ (A1).

Cut 2 squares, 4⅞″ × 4⅞″; cut each square once diagonally to yield 2 half-square triangles (4 total) (B1).

From Fabric 2:

Cut 10 squares, 2½″ × 2½″ (A2).

From Fabric 3:

Cut 2 squares, 4⅞″ × 4⅞″; cut each square once diagonally to yield 2 half-square triangles (4 total) (B3).

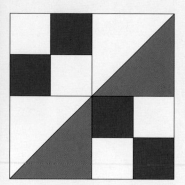

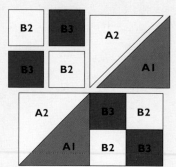

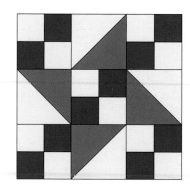

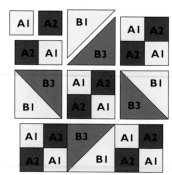

12″

6″

Whidbey Star

This block is assembled using the Flip and Sew method (page 66).

Cutting

12″ Block

From Fabric 1:
Cut 12 squares, 2″ × 2″ (A1).

From Fabric 2:
Cut 24 squares, 2″ × 2″ (A2).

Cut 8 squares, 2″ × 2″ (B).

From Fabric 3:
Cut 4 strips, 2″ × 5″ (C).

From Fabric 4:
Cut 4 strips, 2″ × 6½″ (D).

Whirligig

Cutting

6″ Block

From _each_ of Fabric 1 and Fabric 2:
Cut 1 square, 4¼″ × 4¼″; cut twice diagonally to yield 4 quarter-square triangles (A1 and A2).

From Fabric 3:
Cut 2 squares, 3⅞″ × 3⅞″; cut each square once diagonally to yield 2 half-square triangles (4 total) (B).

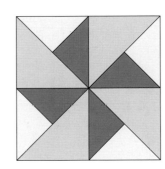

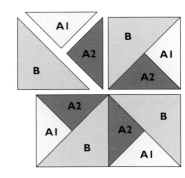

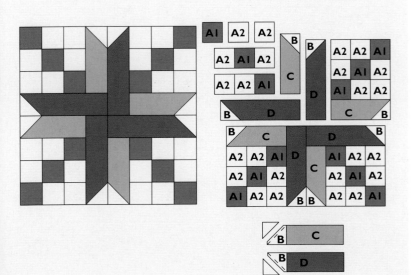

Exchange Paperwork:
SAMPLE FORMS FOR A SUCCESSFUL EXCHANGE

QUILTERS' GUIDELINES FORM

CONTACT INFORMATION

Name: _____

Address: _____

Phone: _____   Mobile: _____

Email: _____   Fax: _____

Theme of quilt, style, mood, feeling I wish to convey: _____

_____

Fabric inventory in container: _____

I do _____ / do not _____ want fabric added to my project.

Types of fabrics/fibers, colors, and styles of fabric that may be added to my quilt: _____

_____

Background specifications: _____

Favorite blocks: _____

Dates of exchange: _____

BLOCK LOG

1ST QUILTER

Name: _____

Address: _____

Phone: _____

Email: _____

Blocks and sizes: _____

2ND QUILTER

Name: _____

Address: _____

Phone: _____

Email: _____

Blocks and sizes: _____

3RD QUILTER

Name: _____

Address: _____

Phone: _____

Email: _____

Blocks and sizes: _____

4TH QUILTER

Name: _____

Address: _____

Phone: _____

Email: _____

Blocks and sizes: _____

5TH QUILTER

Name: _____

Address: _____

Phone: _____

Email: _____

Blocks and sizes: _____

RESOURCES
Sources for Products Referenced

FOR QUILTING SUPPLIES:

Cotton Patch Mail Order
3405 Hall Lane, Dept. CTB
Lafayette, CA 94549
(800) 835-4418
(925) 283-7883
Email: quiltusa@yahoo.com
Website: www.quiltusa.com

In the Beginning
8291 Lake City Way N.E.
Seattle, WA 98115
(206) 523-8862

Note: Fabric manufacturers discontinue fabrics regularly. Exact fabrics shown may no longer be available.

For information about thread:
Robison-Anton Textiles
P.O. Box 159
Fairview, NJ 07022
Website: www.robison-anton.com

For pretreated fabric sheets:
Color Textiles
9030 Sahara
Box 198
Las Vegas, NV 89117
(612) 382-0013
Website: www.colortextiles.com

Milliken & Company
Spartanburg, SC
Email: info@printedtreasures.com
Website: www.milliken.com

For information about printing and scanning on fabric:
Hewlett-Packard Company
Website: www.hp.com/go/quilting/book

For permission-free photos and clip art:
Dover Publications
31 East 2nd Street
Mineola, NY 11501-3582
Fax: (516) 294 -9758
Website: www.doverpublications.com

For your nearest Husqvarna Viking dealer:
Husqvarna Viking
Website: www.husqvarnaviking.com

Helpful Books and Tools

Quick & Easy Block Tool. Edited by Liz Aneloski and Kandy Petersen. Lafayette, CA: C&T Publishing, 2003.

Photo Fun: Print Your Own Fabric for Quilts & Crafts. The Hewlett-Packard Company. Edited by Cyndy Lyle Rymer. Lafayette, CA: C&T Publishing, 2004.

More Photo Fun: Exciting New Ideas for Printing on Fabric for Quilts & Crafts. The Hewlett-Packard Company, Cyndy Lyle Rymer and Lynn Koolish. Lafayette, CA: C&T Publishing, 2005.

Embroidery Collections

These and other embroidery collections are available at your local participating Husqvarna Viking and/or Pfaff sewing machine dealer.

My Favorite Quilt Designs, by M'Liss Rae Hawley, Disk Part #756 253300, *inspira* collection, multiformat CD-ROM.

Spring View, by M'Liss Rae Hawley, Disk Part #756 255100, *inspira* collection, multiformat CD-ROM.

Kimono Art, by M'Liss Rae Hawley, Disk Part #756 259800, *inspira* collection, multiformat CD-ROM.

Candlewicking, Embroidery 46, by Karen McAuliffe, Husqvarna Viking.

Shimmering Paisleys, Disk Part #556 252300, *inspira* collection, multiformat CD-ROM.

Paisley, Embroidery 134, by Margit Grimm, Husqvarna Viking.

Tropical Flowers, Disk Part #756 257600, *inspira* collection, multiformat CD-ROM.

African Arts, Embroidery 37, Husqvarna Viking.

Oriental Fantasy, by Bob Decker, Disk Part #756 258100, *inspira* collection, multiformat CD-ROM.

Hearts, EZ Sew Designs, Disk Part #756 101000, multiformat CD-ROM.

ABOUT THE AUTHOR

Front row (l to r): Barbara Higbee-Price, Peggy Johnson, M'Liss Rae Hawley, Vicki DeGraaf, Susie Kincy.
Back row (l to r): Stacie Johnson, Barbara Dau, Louise James, John James, Anastasia Riordan, Marie L. Miller, Carla Zimmermann, Annette Barca.

M'Liss Rae Hawley is an accomplished quilting teacher, lecturer, embroidery and textile designer, and best-selling author. She conducts workshops and seminars throughout the world. As the author of seven books, including *Phenomenal Fat Quarter Quilts* (2004) and *Get Creative with M'Liss Rae Hawley* (2005), and the originator of numerous innovative designs, M'Liss is constantly seeking new boundaries to challenge her students while imparting her enthusiasm and love for the art of quilting. Although her new PBS television series, *M'Liss's Quilting World*, is in production, M'Liss continues to create fabric with coordinating embroidery collections, write books, and create patterns for *McCall's Quilting* magazine. She likes to break quilting down to the basics to show students that quilting can be easy and fun at any level of skill. M'Liss and her husband, Michael, live on Whidbey Island, Washington, in a filbert orchard. Michael is also a best-selling author and the sheriff of Island County. Their son, Alexander, is in the Marine Corps, and their daughter, Adrienne, is in college. Michael and M'Liss share their home with five dachshunds and three cats.

Great Titles
from  C&T PUBLISHING

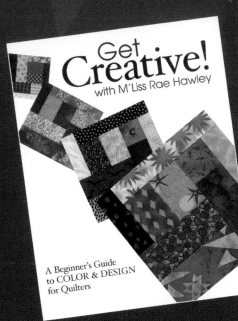